THE
PROPHET

DECIPHER YOUR PAST
RECIPHER YOUR FUTURES

GAY LE

The Prophet
Decipher Your Past Recipher Your Futures

Copyright © 2020 by Gay Le.

Paperback ISBN: 978-1-952982-09-5
Ebook ISBN: 978-1-952982-10-1

All rights reserved. No part in this book may be produced and transmitted in any form or by any means, electronic, or mechanical, including photocopying, recording, or by any information storage and retrieval system, without permission in writing from the copyright owner.

The views expressed in this work are solely those of the author and do not necessarily reflect the views of the publisher hereby disclaims any responsibility for them.

Published by Green Sage Agency   07/28/2020

Green Sage Agency
1-888-366-9989
inquiry@greensageagency.com

TABLE OF CONTENTS

Introduction vii

Chapter 1   Preparation For Seminar 1

Chapter 2   Seminar: Gift Of Death 4

Chapter 3   Life At The Bay 22

Chapter 4   Meeting Roxy 31

Chapter 5   Half Day Seminar 35

Chapter 6   First Break 48

Chapter 7   Second Break 57

Chapter 8   Roxy's Revelations 68

Chapter 9   Living Their Path 76

Chapter 10   Teaching The Path 82

Chapter 11   Creating Perdition 99

Chapter 12   Forging The Path 109

Chapter 13   Perceptional Joy 113

Chapter 14   Jai's Final Tour 141

Part 2

The Druidess

Chapter 15   Hiring Jason 147

Chapter 16   Clash With Destiny 154

Chapter 17   Roxy's Treatment 161

Chapter 18   Anniversary Party 163

Chapter 19	Difference Of Opinion	166
Chapter 20	Roxy's Private Pain	176
Chapter 21	Here Comes The Bride	181
Chapter 22	Wretched Heartache	185
Chapter 23	Welcome Home Jai	189
Index Of Images Pixabay		195

INTRODUCTION

My name is Gay Le. I have studied hypnotherapy since the mid-nineties along with many varied forms of spiritual philosophy. I am recognised in spiritual circles for my platform and counselling work since I was twenty. My passion is past life regression and life between life experiences. In the last seven years I have added the study of narcissism to my research. Society believes this syndrome is environmental however, when you are allowed to add reincarnation to the equation, the consequences of their actions both as perpetrator and victim enhances the algorithm. In an age of computer technology, I have adapted the binary matrix theory to my research, expanding the intellect out of medieval doctrines to the unlimiting expansive consciousness of the future. By modifying our principles of the past that are victimising our potential, we have the ability to create more productively.

All through my life I have been doctrinated with the religious beliefs that we are separated from a God or the creator of the universe, but nothing could be further from the truth. Godness flows through every cell within our body and is an intelligence far beyond our reasoning.

We would not exist without it and it would not exist without us. This is the oneness of all things.

To explain that in a more recognisable manner; in a droplet of blood is over fifty billion cells. Extract one of those cells and within it is another fifty billion cells. Extract again there is another fifty billion cells and so it continues, each one is a duplicate of the original. This continues forever, there is no beginning and there is no end. Within each one of those miniscule cells is the original binary code of creation in fractal form.

To add to the equation, there is a cell responsible for the generating of the liver every six weeks and its demise six weeks later. It too has billions upon billions of cells within it, forging its destination through the Law of attraction. The history of this cell was predetermined over more than 700 billion years ago. However, our liver didn't exist then, this the is the god power. The cell will continue into the next seven billion years continuing on its journey to an unknown destiny with the same intention, and it is that destiny that will forge it forward.

This is how it works. We like all things are immortal.

As humans we started over 200000 years ago. We had no intellectual intelligence that would inform us that we would progress to a nuclear technological computer age, but we advanced regardless.

The Laws of the universe are why this occurs; karma, Law of attraction and the Law of attachment.

The transitions occur like this. Throughout every person's body are billions of cells all holding the same form of binary information defining them as human. Your binary separates you from animal, vegetable and mineral and the environment, water, land and forestry. However, we are one with the overall matrix of all things, so, we are designed to comply with all of them, this is the oneness of all things. Our planet is then one with the entire matrix of the universe. This is the cosmic algorithm.

We like the cell, exist within a cocoon of our own consciousness. No one outside of us are capable of touching us emotionally. They may touch, abuse, make love, kill, but your inner emotions belong to you, and through your true emotional intent you create your future lives. Your perception, based upon your allegiances to your past obligations, will establish the cause of the circumstance occurring before you. Then you will emotionally react to it.

The emotion doesn't really exist. It is simply a response to your surrounding circumstances. You created an emotional impasse. The emotion did not exist until you reacted to it.

Karma is not a judge; it is a response. It will automatically transcribe your newly created emotion into the binary of your DNA for you to personify in your life. The law of attachment which is a force within every cell of your body, will absorb that new binary information and you physically become that emotion. You wear it as your outer garment, your body of history. Everything you think, do and say is defined from this new emotional formation. You echo your creation throughout your entire body. The Law of attraction now matches you to every identical binary rippling through the universe for you to experience in this life and the next. Every word you say is not for the people you are talking to; it is information instructing you of your emotional status and the true intent behind it.

I could never understand why women were always subject to continuous abuse for over 200000 years. Why has it taken over 20000 centuries to finally start standing up and fighting for the rights of women, children and others. It was through the anatomical dividing of the cells that this information was revealed.

When you are accosted by someone, and they are being contentious in your face; what is exposed is the disagreeable emotion displayed by the intent of both parties. This reaction has united both parties as one.

One may be offending and the other may be defending but both parties are in victim mode creating from the same victimising emotion of, rage, anger, malice, lies or hatred. The parties are echoing each other by personifying the same emotion. One is yin, one is yang, but the energy created is the same. The parties are mirroring each other.

When a male, narcissistically abuses a female on a continuous basis; each reproachful and abusive thought word and action is slowly being defined in his binary DNA by karma for him to experience in a future life. In his next life he will return as the victim of the same massive abuse by a narcissistic perpetrator. This female hasn't the courage to stand up to fight for the rights of women for it is too busy defending itself against the narcissistic abuse of the perpetrator. Her fight against her oppressor is now emotionally deeming her new path as a violent arrogant male narcissist again. The emotion still doesn't exist; however, it is a newly conceived emotional reaction that creates the ongoing path.

That has always been the challenge. When the male was been reincarnated as a female it was a victimised narcissistic male inside a female body, so she reacted to the injustice of the male abuse thus, recreating another narcissistic male in a male body again for her to experience and this is their historical path.

We can only alter the perception of the female's station when we are in the female body, acting as a female. We must learn to refrain from standing up to any injustice as it is in the fighting that empowers the narcissistic emotion. We have to learn how to allow life to exist without our reaction. We now see what our reactions looks like. We've seen the results surrounding us and it simply isn't good enough. The fear factor of the world, has been created by this narcissistic dominant anxiety and there is only one way to walk away from it.

We are still capable of creating from our own inner loving power in the same way we create our disdain however, due to our past life affiliations, these outcomes will always be painful expression of our past allegiances. It isn't our dreams we create; it is the underlying emotional attachments from past life passions that determine your path. Your loved ones, friends, work colleagues, enemies, in front of you, will inform you of your underlying emotions, for, through the law of attraction, they will be mirroring you.

When we re-connect to us, we will be free of all the victimising restrictions that we have created to hurt us and our world.

Nothing you say harms or hurts others, it only hurts and harms you.

Everything you think do and say is for you, no one else.

We are connected to our higher consciousness which is connected to its higher consciousness and like the cells within our blood it goes on forever. Each life time we unknowingly raise our conscious awareness. This is defined by our world's progress.

We can manifest with our imagination by using our thoughts, words and actions along with our emotional intent. My objective is to explain, to you how you, when you learn how to recognise the victim mode in which you exist, you have the power to say "NO," freeing yourself, then, personifying yourself in a new body as self-love and self-empowerment.

You allow others to walk their path; you allow the world to be as it is, you even walk with them but you do not have to become engaged in their victimising paths of oppression.

You smile. You laugh. You write your own music and dance to your own song.

There's a song written in 1966 by the Youngbloods. "Let's get together" The last verse says.

"You have the key to love and fear in the palm of your trembling hand. Just one key unlocks them both; it's there at your command"

I'm going to alter that. "You have the key to vanquisher or victim in the palm of your trembling hands, just one key unlocks them both; what is your plan?

Gay Le

CHAPTER 1

PREPARATION FOR SEMINAR

There was a crowd gathered on the street as the ambulance arrived, but word on the street was it was too late. What could they do? He simply walked out in front of the car from behind the bus. Curiosity and panic are defining the area. Police are arriving to hold the onlookers back. Swiftly they contain the area so they can investigate. Was it an accident or something more sinister?

The police start questioning by standers. They need to put a proper perspective on the picture. Photos are taken of the crowd, the traffic and the offender who claims, "This guy just came from out of nowhere and he didn't see him." A sheet is placed over the victim and he is rushed away swiftly. The area cleaned up as quickly as possible. Things slip back into the normal pace easily. By all appearances this is marked as a tragic accident.

Jai is in the crowd as well. He arrived after the accident. He saw the panic in the people but he also saw the victims astral body drift backwards and skywards. It turned and floated away peacefully. It wasn't distressed or shocked at its death; that was unusual. He was no victim. He meant for this to happen. Jai walks away swiftly in his hoodie with his hand tucked warmly in his pockets out of the chilled air.

In the prelife plan the offender agreed to assist the victim to achieve his death this way. Jai understood this, however, the path of the victim now will be one of remorse and regret, and that has to do with something he needed to relive. The pain is simply information explaining why it occurred.

"Good luck with your journey mate; not one I would have chosen, but you had a reason" he thought as he vanished down the alley away from the crowd.

He too has work to do. He has a presentation to prepare for on the weekend and has to perform for those who want readings for families who want answers. His work is not taken seriously by the establishment but he has a solid following and Alex his friend, who is his very money-orientated manager, who is strictly business, has a meeting with him about the set up.

Before he prepares for work, he wants to reschedule a meeting with Jesse his guru associate and co educator who also teaches about higher quantum consciousness. They have a joint business that deals with deep hypnotherapy and all trance worthy experiences, ranging from natural to deep meditations, past life regressions and life between life experiences to non-drug healing. He and his associate enjoy their work due to its uniqueness and it gives them the lifestyle they want to follow their unusual lives independently.

Around 1.75cm tall with dark curly hair and deep ebony eyes he dons a dark mystic appeal which adds to the popularity in his performances. His added sense of humour balances what could be a droll and sad evening. Many come to see his performances looking for answers to the voids in their lives. He explains prelife plans and how we do deliberately put them in place to assist us in our many varied and difficult experiences.

This tragic accident he saw will become part of an acquisitions for training and acquiring a higher level of learning. He feels he has a predetermined path and he aware of his prelife plan and walks it steadfastly.

He was always taunted in his childhood for being an oddball, weird and different. His quirks didn't create fights but he was ostracised and lived his life mostly as a loner. He found interest in other agendas outside the normal class fundamentals and grew up thinking outside of the box.

As he grew, he expanded his mindfulness to higher and higher levels of consciousness and researched many different religious belief systems. His life had been surrounded by many and varied forms of abuse and this also forged his young path.

With two disastrous marriages under his belt and one son whom he adores and who now as an adult follows in his father's footsteps in his business. He lives an unexciting life; but he was ordained the prophet by his audience who saw his philosophies and healing capabilities as a godsend.

He saw his life as his lessons from his past and was able to condone all the unjustifiable actions of those around him as his past life misdemeanours. Through his acts of criticism and judgement he now has to undergo the same actions, for in reality he created them.

This philosophy had evolved from his life between life and past life regressions experience as he was able to recognise the personification of his personal emotional karma. He published his first book based on his unique philosophies and this made him a headliner with his performances.

Christened Jai Tagore at birth he had both Indian and Polynesian heritage and he physically possessed the beauty of both worlds. Being born without life it was a struggle to bring him into this world. When he finally arrived, he required medical help and remained in hospital for several weeks.

Later in his teenage years he had a very strong affiliation with the afterlife and the reason was because of his birth. This became an obsession. Once he discovered hypnotherapy it strongly became his passion.

Jai had finally developed his ambitions and was achieving goals both spiritually and materially. He was now old enough to accept his lot in life and find contentment in his walk forward to a more pleasant future life. He felt confident he was successful and was on the right path.

CHAPTER 2

SEMINAR: GIFT OF DEATH

Saturday morning came and there was still much to be done for the night's performance and Jai was still rushing about trying to make last minute arrangements and get everything ready and organised. The street was abuzz with hustling and bustling with everyone in their own world of importance.

A newcomer to town was coming in the opposite direction and keeping pace with her crowd, while Jai was racing toward her. The collision was evident but they swiftly veered passed each other while the universe magnetically pulled the slightest touch of hands and finger tips causing a crack in the dimension which opened up a past life portal for both of them.

She spun around on her heels and fell to the ground. She slid around the corner to escape the bustle and he was jolted to stop as if he'd been hit in the chest. He caught a visual of her only for a second. She had short golden cropped blond hair and a long coat. He had to stop still for a moment. In front of him was a vision of a past experience.

A young girl, a teenage child in front of him with long golden hair braided with a wreath of flowers and he felt high sexual tension throughout this body with an intense desire to kiss her. His hand was slowly starting to embrace her face when he saw a huge golden nugget ring on the thumb of his left hand. Then the vision was gone.

Jai turned around searching for her, bobbing up and down over the crowd but she had vanished in to the throngs of people all forging forward like flooded water.

Jai returned to the studio where Jesse had rounded off another meditation tape that was ready to edit. Jai started acting out his frustration by slamming down his keys and paper work on the table.

"Do I ask?" queried Jesse, as he kept on working about the office so he could finish his work. It was Saturday and he wanted to go home. He really didn't want a long drama that would have him going round and round in circles. Jesse too was of Polynesian decent, long black hair tied into braid. Around 1.80 cm more solid build with the beauty of the islands and a very deep mellow voice.

"What do you do when you've had a vision of some sort about you?" Jai pause for a second "or at least I think it was about me."

"Wait for more information" responded Jesse as he started packing up the last of his equipment.

"That's it?"

"Yep that's it" replied Jesse as he started exiting the building. "You got nothin to work with."

He closed the door behind him.

Jai paced a little longer and finally agreed to himself "you've got nothing to work with," shrugged his shoulders and started preparing the last of morsels of information needed for the night's performance.

Tonight, his address was about the loss of children and how they have prepared this event to occur and it isn't the barbaric act of loss as foretold by many archaic principles. He'd performed this address before and received high accolades, so he was asked to reperform it for others to hear and experience.

He put his manager to work to advertise in all the appropriate places so he would have a full house with another very receptive audience. He had work to do. He put the incidence of the mornings happening behind him.

The venue was sold out and held 1000 people and there would be an interval. He had his power point ready; his screen was set up to display enlightening quotes to assist audience with their healing. It would also display quotes from great philosophers and teachers throughout the centuries. They have been artistically prepared to create the greatest impact.

He checked his microphones volume and all the appropriate settings for the audio around the venue. It has two large screens one on each side of the stage for the inscriptions with the small one behind him producing a video image of him on stage. The video and books would be sold after the performance outside the live venue, for customer's pleasure.

The venue is ready, now he has to prepare himself. It would be a hot night in this venue especially on stage as all the air conditioning would be more for the audience so his crème tailored shirt and dark slacks. Hair washed and left slightly wet to keep it controlled and that should do it.

He was pleased with his appearance as he didn't want anything too high starched or at the same time to risqué. Yes, that was satisfactory considering the heat.

He was ready. The venue was packing as the motivating music pulsed through the theatre and he was pacing backwards and forwards, collecting his thoughts. This was his quiet time before the show and no interruptions were appreciated. His computer was placed on the dais and the video camera was placed in the centre of the forum with the audience. All was ready.

He was told he had 10 minutes. Deep breathing now and calming methods were required to calm the inner nerves. A quick gargle of scotch for his voice and he began walking towards the stage.

The announcer motivates the audience and they are up on their feet anticipating the night's presentation. Everyone including Jai had high expectation for the night's performance as he upped his pace and walked out onto the stage amid a huge audience accolade from his admirers.

Nerves were gone now, they wanted him. They wanted his philosophies as they cheered his appearance.

He raises his hands up in appreciation and speaks into his collar microphone. "Good evening and welcome to a night that should prove to be both entertaining and thought provoking. My Name is Jai Tagore. Yes, although I am Polynesian, my father's father came from India. So, yes, I was rubbished at school. Well what's in a name? Well for starters, my name is now famous and theirs isn't." The audience enjoyed his humour and reacted nicely. "And no, I'm not related to the great guru"

Jai then went on to explain who he was and how he had chosen his career path. Then he started opening up with the audience and asking if any had experienced the death of a young loved one. Several hands went up. "How many of you have lost a younger loved one in their middle age?" A few more hands went up.

"The only difference between these deaths is the time period for us on earth. Death is a highly significant part of life. It is a deliberate part of our life plan and as a tool we use it for many different results.

Before we start, let a couple of things be known. This seminar is about loss of loved ones from children to adults who are your children regardless of age. Now a couple of statistics that are never considered.

Marriage is a man-made concept." As he walks across the stage, he points his finger over the audience's heads, "annnnd, the minute the female enters puberty all her children start entering into the world.

You may not have them for years even decades but your destiny for them and your individual partners has already started, no accidents."

On the side screens is a huge quote is displayed:

DEATH IS A PREPLANNED FUNCTION OF EACH EXISTENCE

"Let's start at the beginning. One thing that plays an important component in their departing is the age when they left.

The first of the deaths that cripple many mothers is the miscarriage. For any sufferers here tonight my deepest condolences." He paused for a few seconds. "Both you and your child agreed to this event. Firstly, the child wasn't always a child; and secondly the child had an agenda that needed your assistance.

The child may have to acquire the DNA binary so it can be attracted to your family at a later date. If this is the case these children are easily detected when they return.

Unlike the rest of us whose every gene is absolutely riddled with past life judgemental binaries and allegiances caught up in our DNA which defines our personalities later in all our lives, these beautiful people usually arrive without any form of judgement or criticism of anyone.

They have a genteel kindness and genuine non-judgemental attitude to others. This personality displays itself at a very early age. They usually appear as one your grandchildren. Another clue is they have acquired the same DNA as the older child before the miscarriage. That child will usually become the parent or grandparent." He paused and looked at his audience and asked. "Still with me? I haven't lost you yet? Great," He continued.

"Secondly the miscarried child may have another agenda and that may be to clean their own slate.

If an existence is to be one of unjust homicide or malice that the soul does not wish to participate in, it can choose to abort. If they do not have the courage to do it, they will influence the mother to want an abortion, and sometimes this is carried out. Nothing is a mistake, except the enormous guilt.

Even though there is judgement against abortion, if you are in an area where it is illegal and protested against; you chose to be in that area for that reason. When a country purports a law against injustice believed it to be god's will it isn't, it is man's laws; however, before you came here you all agreed to it. You then chose to live there so this action would be decided for you on earth, even though you orchestrated it before you came here over two hundred to a thousand years ago. That's freaky isn't it? You thought it was just before you came here.

You prepared these escapades centuries in advance, preparing grandparents, parents, relations, and your children. You are part of a lineage and they play an important part in the ongoing continuum of all your lives. They may not always be the same lineage either.

I personally support a woman's choice. My argument is this conduct was also your choice before you came here. So, don't get caught in the politics and judge others this will come back to you badly and you don't want that. Your anger to the injustice either way, for or against, will be deemed as your future path.

I have a friend who enjoys putting me down and he said to me to stop contradicting religions or politics because in my next life I'll come back as a white pompous ass religious politician." He raises his eye brows and rolls his eyes as the audience laughed. "So, be careful what you say," he laughed and continued. "Be careful who you verbally hate, unless you want to literally walk in their shoes in your next existence. You may see yourself as at the top of the ladder and them below you but in your next existence you will be on the rung below them but, that's another story for another night.

The second the child enters the womb to repair past judgements as they are supposed to, but instead of staying and being completely imprinted by the dimensional binaries that are unacceptable to them, they choose to leave with a pure clean slate to return to future life of happiness.

You agreed to help them accomplish this.

There are many agendas for miscarriages my point here is, there is always a much higher purpose here and it was never deemed to hurt anyone, especially the beautiful mothers who feel the anguish the most. You all agreed to the outcome so all could be happy.

The side screens alter;

NOTHING IS DONE TO HARM YOU. ALL IS DONE OUT OF LOVE.

To me that makes you the bravest of beings, and to quote St Francis, 'it is in the giving that you receive.' You will receive the highest of accolades and no one is more deserving."

"After the show I will be in the foyer if you have any questions. I'll be more than happy to talk some more on this.

Next is cot deaths, early deaths, and childhood accidents; these again are pre-ordained requests by the children and agreed upon by all participants. In one of my life between life hypnotherapy sessions I asked this question. The reason I asked was, up to that date I had been informed that a soul never enters a baby who is going to die. That to me appeared unacceptable so I asked.

The response was completely different and made more sense.

And I asked "why wasn't this information given before?" The response was to do with the higher level of quantum open-ness from the inquirer. That also opened a door to another question and the answer was the same. The interpretation of the life between life session pends on the open quantum-ness of the inquirer. That altered many of the fundamentals I'd been taught but it opened up our research further.

These beautiful babies have dual tasks, also, pending on the age of the child at death will determine when they return either as grandchildren or great grandchildren. These children as new borne or a little older have to resolve issues with the parent or loved one so as a small child they experience unconditional love. This is the greatest healer of all past obstacles. This is the healing they require; now you will love them forever and all past life wrongdoings by both of you or all others has been redeemed.

They may have made hasty judgements against you as parents in a previous life and didn't get the opportunity to make amends and that decision has to be remedied so they can return to fulfil their true mission later. It may be a small blockage but it will prevent them from being loved completely. They may have become separated from their loved one, now they can return later in the same or different lineage to enjoy the love of their loved one. In some cases, these children as adults marry soul mates much older than themselves, why, because they arrived late so to speak. They were busy.

Suicide by children; this is another devastating death to have to deal with. Again, my deepest commiserations to anybody who has had to experience this heart rendering pain. Suicides of all descriptions are truly based on healing past life pain between all participants. The pain appears to be the driving force behind each experience.

In this situation there is a lot of victimisation and guilt, to clarify this pain. This information is feedback only. You need to know why this happened. The emotional trauma you are feeling is the emotion you need to experience to inform you of the emotional trauma that caused it. It is this very emotion you caused them in the past. Now it has been balanced. It is information only. You are not meant to hang onto it and deem a future path with it. Now you let it go. You have to remember the love your shared not the pain and the move on. It was an act of love. Why didn't you see the signs, why didn't the child open up to you or to someone who could help? The horrible answer is; they weren't meant to. This was their path. It had a higher purpose of healing and pending on the age will determine whether they return to the same lineage or move onto another.

These souls have a determined resolution to an issue again that needs to be resolved. Usually the age they pass at and the period just before their passing is the same time frame this incident occurred in their past life. All the anguish and pain the child had to go through had to be repeated by the child so all participants could resolve the past life issue and now you all can move on to a more loving goal.

The side screen alters;

NOTHING IS A MISTAKE. ALL IS DONE FOR THE HIGHEST GOOD OF EVERYONE

The constant barraging by menacing others, the loss of something out of their control, ill health, all these pressures are a predetermined request that has to push the victim to the limits to crush them. The timing of the death will determine the amount of past life judgement they will take with them.

If they aren't quite an adult and in spiritual teachings the age of maturity is around 30 not the age of an adult; it means they have not acquired all the binary information from their past life. In some cases, they leave with an entirely new clean slate. The pain enforced by others may have cleansed all their past injustices, now they have a clean slate. Now they will become 'new souls,' cool hey?" He pauses to take a drink.

"You as a parent or friend have given them the opportunity to be happier than they have ever been before. You offered your assistance to help them to overcome their arduous path. Part of that was to not be available to materialistically save them.

By being invisible you gave them eternal joy for future lives. You offered to share in their joy. So, if this is a means to attain higher happiness how can it be a sin or a misdemeanour? However, refrain from producing emotional judgements against this form of action or you will follow suit to find out.

There is another form of suicide and that is in adults. Again, it has been preordained. The suicide is simply the act; it is the emotional intent behind all action that creates the ongoing pain. This was most likely created from their judgement of others in a past life. Judgemental others call them cowards, selfish and cannot understand why they would want to hurt the ones left behind. Now he knows. This was their predetermined destiny. Through creating an emotion due to someone doing the same thing in the past they actually created the same emotion within them for them to experience, in its entirety to the full extent of their judgement. Now it is done, let it go or you too will follow suit. That is the ongoing reincarnational continuum or history repeating itself.

"We'll take a break now and when we return, I'll tell you the blessing of death by disease and the worst of all deaths, murder. There's a supper outside so see you in 20 minutes."

There was a standing ovation as he leaves the stage and a lot of murmuring as they move outside to get refreshment and freshen up.

Jai went back stage to his fridge and pulled out a nice cold drink. Although there was water on stage, this work dehydrates you. He wiped his face with fresh water and sat for a while to catch his breath. Several of the stage hands came back to see if he was happy with the process so far and he was. He questioned about the DVD was he moving too fast, was the light okay? Alex came in quite exuberant about how it's turning out.

The stage hands went back and prepared for part two of the recording of the DVD. They played some of their meditation music which they placed on display for purchase later.

The twenty minutes seem to pass so quickly and it was time to return. Jai changed his gear into a light blue shirt and another more comfortable pair of daks. Water through the hair quick dry and he was ready again. Deep breath and out he went.

The audience gave him a warm welcome back. Some stragglers were still trying to find their seats so he waited patiently.

"While some are still trying to find their seats, I'll ask if any one has any questions." A voice echoed from the audience. "If you miscarried the first child and there is not child to follow?"

"Good question and the answer is still the same as the miscarriage of the child as with an older brother or sister only this time they are acquiring the binary of either parent. This happened to my sister. The resemblance is uncanny. Our grandmother miscarried her first son and through my younger sister who is her granddaughter, she gave birth to a genuine replica of our grandfather. He was deaf in the same ear and loved maths. This child utilised maths in his work and has the sweetest nature, but he is our grandfather's duplicate. However, he is without any form of judgement or past life criticism in his personality. Wisdom beyond his years; amazing kid.

The other one I missed is miscarriages when you are trying IVF. It is the same for them. All of you have chosen to participate in these events. But with some of these they do not return to the same time line or lineage, they can turn up as a nephew or niece. But this one has yet to be asked and proven, but they aren't too far away.

Okay, screen and action. Diseases and murder, which do you want first?

Murder?" He gives a giggle "interesting crowd."

The audience responds.

"YES! You allow murder too!" the audience laughs.

The side screen alters.

THEY WEREN'T ALWAYS CHILDREN

"Oooh" he mocks as he looks at the screen and rubs his hands together. The audience responds.

"That's the most difficult concept to accept. When you hear of a murder where a child is involved, it is an unacceptable crime. Be it child abuse, paedophilia, acts of terror, war, genocide and impoverishment throughout the world; when a child is the front runner to the campaign it is unacceptable behaviour.

Your judgements of these actions will be your demise. The first thing to recognise is, the action between the victim and the perpetrator is between them. When they put this action into play it is a plan between the two people involved. Game over. Once this is done, the exercise between them is finished.

However, your judgement of the situation will keep it occurring and you and your criticism will influence the future outcome of *your* lives. It may take four or five life times but the drawing factor, the magnetising force will be the murder of you; act over.

This incident was placed in front of you because of a previous judgement. You criticised. That emotion behind that criticism will manifest into your persona through your DNA. Now you are on the river Styx and it won't stop until the task is complete according to your accusations. Now with today's knowledge if you have or are experiencing this dimension you can now alter the outcome, that's why you are here.

When this plan is put into place to continue the ongoing actions, they are followed by judges, jurors, police and public. Now it may not be the same actions of unacceptable behaviour, but it will be the same emotional impact. It may not be a world war, but it may be a civil war, or street protests that last for months.

The child has already existed in worlds of war or genocide where they were the perpetrator and this time, they have to experience the pain and suffering they incurred on others by expressing their hatred of their victims. To be killed as the child finishes the entire exercise and they leave with a clean slate and their karma balanced.

The perpetrator will experience the same pain in their next existence and he will get the opportunity to clean his slate as well. This is the path they have been drawn into, due to incorrect emotional perceptions in their past. The judges will step up to be the perpetrators to then be killed then have a clean slate and so the reincarnations continuum endures.

It used to be called the lemniscate or the infinity sign; what goes around comes around. Some may have one life left to experience till they have a clean slate and others may have five or six before they get theirs, but all paths lead back to the nirvana of all things. Nirvana is the beginning and endings of all things. That's my perception.

Here's the 'get out of jail free card'. Once you recognise how the River Styx flows you can get out of the boat at any time during the experience. You simply have to alter your perspective about the circumstances.

Murder of a child who gets a king punch outside a pub; has an over dose from a drink at a festival; gets killed in a car accident; the list is endless; all under the same brush. The emotional drama reflects their

The Prophet

previous opinion of similar situation, now they experience that same emotional drama. These children may be amazing and their parents find it difficult to lose such a treasure, but if the parent hang onto any revengeful anger they will experience the exact same lifestyle in the exact same way they expressed it. Every word you say is writing the script.

Now you are progressing. Can you see why these children would ask you to participate in this experience?" There's a murmur from the audience. "Yes, it has a lot to do with the unconditional love of everything. The family again and the child has to revaluate a past life situation and by doing it this way they all leave with an abundance of that unconditional love.

If the parents don't judge and learn to allow, they too will experience abundance of joy knowing they played a huge part in the joyful experience of the child's soul. By allowing the peace and understanding, you have given the child the most exalting gift, you in return will receive the same in this life This is what Francis of Assisi means when he says: "it is in the giving that you receive." You have given the ultimate gift to the person you think you have lost.

To have a clean slate and be able to start again. That's like New Year's Eve with fire crackers exploding worldwide.

You did that; you allowed that; so why would you want to put a damper on the situation by misjudging it. Nothing is a mistake nothing is a sin everything is our experience and sometimes the worst of what we see is the most magnificent of all gifts.

It doesn't matter how the original misdemeanour occurred, it is finished; it is between the perpetrator and the victim they are the final two in the experience.

If there is no judgement, no emotion involved, and the perpetrator has to experience a death to clean his slate but there are other methods available to them that don't hurt others. Due to the flow of the dimension all the perpetrators will be redeemed. This is the Law of attraction giving you your hearts desires.

Summary;" He paused and paced back and forth. "The victim judged a death situation 1300 years ago. Their death in this life time is the end game and it was dictated in every lifetime in between. All of them have been experienced in order for them to achieve this final outcome so they too can be redeemed from their original judgement. This is why I call it the river Styx: it pulls you along until it is done.

Now are there any more questions on murder? Basically, it is the same for all. Our job is to realise that all is taken care of and we should learn to mind our own business." A loud voice reaction to his version on justice was questioned.

"No, no, no. Don't misunderstand the supposed injustice?"

Jai take a breath and pauses for a moment.

Securing himself in the centre of the stage he begins. "God, the cosmos, the universe simply is no more. It is simply amazing self-power and love nothing more and it exist within all of us. It allows us to be whatever it takes to make us happy. So, one guy stands up and says I'm going to blow up a boat. God says fine if that make you happy. Then the next person says if you're going to blow up boats, I'm going to stop you. God by not interfering is allowing you to find out for yourself the repercussions of you and your choices. God does not judge us and we shouldn't either but if you insist in breaking civil rules someone is also going to stop you. All contenders are accounted for in the balance of the world and the universe. Your happiness is the most important thing but if you don't know how to achieve it, others will help you achieve it even if it means bumping you off.

There's a story of a young boy whose parent recommended he wear a jacket to football training as it was going to be cold. "No," he responded "he'd be fine." He went to training and on his way home in the car he sat in the back seat freezing, and said, "next time I'll bring a coat." He learnt by his own experience. And had the parents stood an argued with him he would have argued back however, by allowing him to make his own decision there were no further repercussions by anyone.'

By treating others with respect and equality you in turn will receive respect and equality.

Now, when they bump you off, they have allowed the justice system the legal system to be set up for them to experience the injustice. The setting up of the justice system was put in place from the other side for the villains to experience. Nothing is an accident. All is exactly as it should be. All I'm saying is that by *judging* you will follow the path of the perpetrator. Beware what you say; you may end up becoming a puritanic politician like me;" he laughed, "You can come and join me in the white house," he pauses and shrugs his shoulders, "well I can't be any worse!" The audience laughs.

"Right the final journey and it is a lovely one but it is a painful one. This is the purest evidence that we request absolute battering to achieve the highest good. Again, it has been established from ongoing emotions that personify you from that perspective.

One of my favourite quotes is Rumi's I use it so often and I'll use it again. *"It is in breaking the heart that we awaken the heart"* Once we bleed, we eradicate the disease of this existence and rise to a higher level of consciousness in this existence and we are able to love everyone and everything unbelievably and unconditionally. It is in the bleeding that you are able to release all the past life angst. I not talking blood. There are several types of awakening some are overwhelmingly fast some are like this one slow. This one is slow because you continuously prevent the awakening from occurring.

Illness comes from a situation of centuries of self-battering, hatred, abuse from both sides of the karmic table. It is what we call 'body history.' Your body replicates all your past life pains and how it attracts more to you. Taking the karmic tumble there is a story in Robert Monroe's second book where a soul is attracted to an earthly dimension, so he enters and in his first life he enjoys the life and life style. So, he is keen to return.

In his next life he is incarnated as a woman in a difficult situation where she kept losing her young children. She lost her husband, then was gang raped by infidels. She died. When she's reincarnated again, she was angry and vengeful and he wanted to be a male retaliating soldier and he was passionately driven to murder all the infidels. This continuous perpetrator verses victim took its toll over many centuries. And in his book, he never experienced love again.

This is what occurs with illnesses. This constant battering and incarcerating of the soul through the judgement of hatred is persecuting us not others. We personify the emotion and it exposes itself through ill health. Each life you return you will have the past life imprints of an illness set within your DNA and your body will display it. All this occurs up to the final stage where you collapse because you can't *fight* it any more. You are incapable of empowering it any more, releasing all forms of lack of control and low self-esteem. The disease is informing you of your lack of control for it controlled you and it was out of control.

If you are an adult you will experience all behaviours that will inform you of these past lives. The people around you will be disruptive and argumentative and out of control. All forms of addictions telling you that they cannot control something. You will endure slave labour because you will want to control others' lives. These actions are telling you to start controlling yours.

Your life will be one where you enjoy controlling your environment by enslaving yourself in your own control preventing yourself from loving yourself. All the people around you will fulfil all your needs to help you become ill. This is your request. Then you will experience the illness and the chemicals of the dimension will assist you to crack your hardened casing open. If you are successful then you should not only celebrate with all your loved ones but with yourself. You've achieved something that has been a huge obstacle for centuries.

If the chemicals don't work this doesn't mean it's a failure. You have still been healed but you will get it upon your return home. This incident occurs when you reincarnate with the disease as a child. This is when you will again recover or die and return as a grandchild. If the child dies it is because the obstacle that had to be rendered was with the relationship the child and the parents had. Now they can all move forward successfully.

When older people have debilitating diseases, it is because of their relationship with themselves throughout their life. In today's times, the miscalculation of attaining wealth over happiness leaves an empty self-relationship and fear. One of the biggest faux pas is when we listen to old cranky leaders who live in fear and lead our countries from this frame of mind. It is detrimental to the world's health.

Illness comes from centuries of build-up of personal fear. Our emotions personify the displeasure then we have to embody it. This is the format of all life.

Everything around you is feedback. It is not punishment or people out to hurt you. It is pure unadulterated data to inform you of the emotion within you that is victimising you and blocking you from achieving your true happiness.

By learning to allow what is happening around you and realising all things are as they should be, because, we actually want it that way so we can move forward, then you too will have to start believing everything is perfect and so are you.

Now for a little story to bind all this. We all truly appear to be bound in an existence of narcissism. When we enter here, according to all the great philosophers we enter a veil. Well that veil is the outer shield of your consciousness and once you enter you cannot see out. Within that veil is all the turbulence of what you are to experience in a type of a cocoon.

Now it gets trickier, if you want to get out, you have to look in. The key to escaping all these experiences is the inner self-love with you. The problem is, our perception says we have to reach out empowering our outer existence of victimisation.

By learning that you are so much more than this dome of narcissistic hatred which encircles you and it deems the way you think, look speak and act. You need to look inside yourself and free yourself from all the victimisation surrounding you and see who you truly are. Once you release all forms of victimisation, that is friends, family, work associates, and lovers, you start loving yourself unconditionally and you experience amazing feelings of self-empowerment and freedom.

If you have health issues it is this narcissistic component of you that you are overindulging. Now with narcissism if it cannot control you, it will control how others perceive you. So, it will set up people to make you feel unworthy, so you overindulge it more and start walking on eggshells.

If you have weight problems and you are over indulging your inner narcissist every time you abandon it; it will return and not only will it abuse you again it will ensure you put on more weight to ensure you won't do it again to confirm you cannot escape.

If you are wrapped up in materialism it is the same as the weight problem. You vie for freedom; it will force its way back and when it comes back it will wrap you up so tight in its dominance that the shield you put around you will stop any form of love from entering. The intensity of the materialism needed is equivalent to the lack of self-empowerment within you.

This circumstance is as bad as people who suffer from obesity. You are all covering yourself so no one can touch you, no one can hurt you again. But it the emotion you created that is hurting you. It will hurt you by attracting the same painful people to you so you will maintain this painful circumstance.

Wouldn't it be nicer to have that unconditional love you deserve? Wouldn't it be nice if someone came and loved you regardless? If they reached into your heart and said you are the most beautiful person they have ever met and they will love you forever, the way you want to be loved.

Reach inside, for that person is there. From there attach yourself to that love of your life. Become that love. Personify that love. They may not be in this life time but they exist. Know that their love for you is above all others.

Cling to that and instead of going through a maze or labyrinth of destruction, a path is paved from you directly to them. Never let go and they and all the things you need to get to them will come to you.

Rumi again, 'what you are looking is looking for you;' the money, new town, new house, new job, all will pave the path to you; you do not have to slave to achieve this. The path is already deemed. All you have to do is walk it.

Let go of your control and all the victimising pain you endure due to the dimension you had to enter because you got lost. You are no good to any one till you are good to you and find your true path then others will follow graciously. Now go out there and build the life you truly want, not the life you have to serve.

Okay that's it folks. Thanks' for coming. I'll be outside in the foyer for signing of books and any questions you have.

You have been a fabulous audience. I hope you have enjoyed tonight as much as I have enjoyed bringing it to you and I look forward to seeing you all soon. My name is Jai Tagore, I'm a reincarnation specialist and a hypnotherapist and I wish a safe journey home and I wish you Goodnight.

He raises both his arms and waves to the audience as he departs the stage. The music fills the theatre.

The stage lights go dim and the lights of the venue turn up. There is stretching and shuffling and moving as the audience starts exiting the venue to the foyer.

He needs to change his shirt again so he slips into another crème one and prepares to enter the foyer. Checks deodorant, hair; has water and walks out into a huge gathering in the foyer that applauds his entrance.

"This will be busy night." He finds his table where he has to sit to sign. He finally sits and take a deep breathe. "Okay how can I help you?" He asks his first fan. She hands him a copy of his book for him to sign. She introduces herself and he autographs her book with a personal inscription just for her. She's impressed as she leaves with a smile.

He is there for about an hour and a half working hard on signing books and answering well-wisher's questions. It's a long night; however, Alex was extremely satisfied. With everyone paid they made a considerable profit.

Jai was happy for him. He just wanted to get his clothes and possessions so he can go home to bed. 'What a day!'

Home was outside the town in a two-bedroom house on some land, not too much. Jai wasn't impressed with too much mowing. It was suitable. Small enough to maintain and big enough to have friends over for a relaxing night of entertainment.

He found his lounge and slumped on it out of exhaustion. Too tired to get a drink yet still wound up from the performance. When he finally gets the strength, he'll have a shower and pass out on his bed. He recollected that woman that morning, why did she appear to be in front of him? Why did he want to kiss her? Who was she?

As Jesse says not enough information. It opens a door to too much speculation. This incident needs more time.

3
CHAPTER

LIFE AT THE BAY

Of a morning Jai would go to the water for his early morning swim, then run home to half an hour on the lightweights, quick shower, quick bacon and eggs and drink for breakfast then to the studio. This had been his regime for many years now. It gave him a clear head kept him focused.

On Sunday this was to be his normal schedule until he was interrupted. He was running up the sand to his towel. Very few people were up at this hour of the morning on Sunday. He thought he was alone. Drying his locks with his towel he stood in the morning sun glowing from moisture dripping from his well-structured body. His heritage tan emphasised his perfectly toned abs and his dark hair accentuated his sensual facial features.

In the fore ground walking toward him was two people known to him and they waited for him to start walking toward them. As the female displayed her appreciation at such a beautiful vision so early in the morning the senior male detective known by the name of Frank decided to take the lead. They started approaching Jai as they had some questions for him regarding the accident the previous week.

"I don't know anything," explains Jai "It was all over by the time I got there, why?" they explained it was routine to check with everyone and they saw his image in their photos. "Am I under suspicion?" he queried as he put on his hoodie. "Come on you guys, I wasn't the only one wearing a hoodie that day; it was freakin cold."

"Look Jai we're not saying anything; it's simply routine questioning."

"Routine my ass; anyway, I thought it was an accident, isn't that what the papers are saying?"

Jai started picking up the pace now in to a small jog,

"Don't believe everything you hear" grunted Frank." I was just wondering if you may know anything more. You know what I mean? "queried Frank rather hesitantly.

"Yep," responded Jai. "He was glad it was over. Does that help.?"

Jai started picking up the pace now. "There's a note Frank, a wallet or a bag, but there's a note. I'm off; we finished here?"

"Yeah get lost." They slowly trudged up the sand bank and Jai headed off ahead of them running on his path home. Frank turned to his offsider "you need a life."

"Are you kidding?" she squawked. "For the last three weeks the only male bodies I seen have been at the morgue. That one is very much alive, wet and delicious. I'll ogle it any day" She giggles and her partner mumbled under his breath "He's old enough to be your father. We went to school together"

She looked at him surprised, "you an' him?"

"Well he was a couple of years younger" he quickly retorted,

"What kindergarten?" she sarcastically replied.

"Funny; coffee?" he asked

"Yeah make yours a double shot." She laughed,

"And I know exactly where I'll shoot it" he mumbled

"Was that a joke Frank, we're doing jokes now?"

They laughed as they climbed the ramp to the newly opened café. Not many cafés opened early on Sundays; this new café was going to rattle some cages.

Jai arrived home did his workout and then continued his morning ritual. Today he would do more research. He would have to go through his tapes that he had created from his past life hypnotherapy sessions not only for himself but some clients as well. This research verified his philosophies of the continuum of lives. He saw the world as divided up into different dimensions and he discovered our past lives were attracted to each individual dimension.

From these tapes he was able to see different connections to each life and the karmic effect applied in them and how they are balancing acts as opposed to punishments. His clients ranged from doctors to housewives to professors at the uni and every single one had a different world to the other. They appeared to be cocooned in their world of their own making and everything occurred to them according to their beliefs.

Jesse and he were qualified practitioners and had equipment that would induce the client into deeper and more reliable states of trance. Many sessions could take a minimum of two hours some up to four hours.

A prelife plan can take several sessions of over three hours each. This was a research clinic and they received sponsor ship and have achieved brilliant results in normal health and healing situations.

The cash flow comes from dietary and cigarette problems.

These are quick one-hour sessions twice a week for two weeks. They have a high success rate because they are not relying completely on human resources. All sessions have to be recorded and they must comply with normal doctor patient confidentiality.

Clients are allowed hypnotherapy tapes to take home to do touch ups if they need it. Many people return to try something new and better, so their reputation and the fact that they don't have to charge a fortune is a benefit.

The morning had been long and it was Sunday, Jai decided to go to check out the new establishments that was serving organic food along with other forms of healthy food. This place was long overdue here; he liked the concept of being able to dine out and eat well.

It was a nice day for a drive so he decided to take his little sports car along the water way for a spin. The café was situated on the water front with both kiosk and dine in. It held a pleasant view of the water and shore front. Jai parked in the shaded parking area behind the café and wanted to have a dine-in chai and maybe something nice to eat.

At the kiosk Jai saw Alex was ordering. He was still in the clothes he wore the night before. Was he just going home? Jai had to laugh; that guy lives on the edge, so totally different to Jai. He was organised, practical and logical but Alex is going to have a husband chase him one day. His reputation preceded him. Many women knew of his badass attitude and found it appealing.

He was a dashing man and strutted his stuff like a man of prestige; very cocky and sure of himself; and a little over confident for Jai, however he could arrange his promotions better than anyone he knew in the business.

Jai entered the café only to be greeted by a very familiar face who he thought worked on the other side of town. Friendly greetings passed and Jai gave his friend Jason his order. As he was about to sit down out of the corner of his eye, he saw the blonde. She was serving drinks to a table.

"Hey Jason, who's the blonde?" he queried as he kept an eye on her.

"That's Roxy. She's the owner. You'd like her. Want an intro?"

"Not today thanks." He watched her moving around delivering the orders to tables.

"She does tarot reads." This caught Jai's attention, "Not like normal tarots, they are connected to past life stuff like yours."

"Past life stuff?" responded Jai

"Yeah that stuff you do only she does it with tarots. She's really good. Maybe I could get her to give you a read?" Jason laughed

Jai leaned into the counter and said agreeably "Maybe you could."

Jai went to find a seat against the back wall so he could watch everything, especially this Roxy.

Roxy served his table quickly and he smiled and said "thank you," as his stomach skipped a beat.

Why would that happen? She was sweetly attractive; she was nice but why would he react to her? This situation was weirder than his usual ones. She did work hard, and the place was busy so she should do well.

He enjoyed the menu and would probably return not only for the food. Jai now knew where she was; he needed a plan of action if he was going to solve this dilemma. A tarot read; no, that really wasn't his style, but it did open a door for conversation.

After he had finished his meal Roxy came to clear his table. She queried if everything was to his satisfaction. He smiled and nodded yes. She left.

'Bloody hell," he chastised to himself. "That's the best you've got. What the f… is up with you? You can't even speak to the woman." He went up to the counter pay his bill. "How'd it go?" Jason asked as he took his credit card.

"Yeah good"

"So, we'll see you again?" asked Jason

"Yeah why not," responded Jai nodding and feeling confident that he would.

"Hey I heard the show last night was a huge success" stated Jason

"How'd you hear that?"

'Alex came in earlier. He did his bloating and boasting as usual, but hey that's great; good on ya… again. Next time let us know we'd like to put in a proposal to cater for it."

Jason returned his credit card with his business card. "Call us"

"I just might do that," responded Jai. 'Now that sounds like a plan.'

Jai was anxious to see Jesse again. His head was buzzing with ideas and ways to overcome all this confusion. But it was still Sunday and Jesse had a rule. Stay away on Sundays.

When they first started their practice Jai would get so excited, he couldn't stop working and he would be at Jesse's house working on his day off. Finally, Jesse exasperatedly stated, "Go home; take a day off; or better still, get out and let me have my day off."

Jai's excitement has calmed down in his older years and now he does respect his dear friend's privacy. He'll inundate him tomorrow, he sniggered to himself.

Jai had a restless night sleep. He had an out of body experience during his dreams. This had become a common occurrence with all the hypnotherapy he had undergone. Many dreams involved his astral body experiences; they never did anything overly adventurous. He read once where this form of astral traveller are light healers.

That made sense to him as sometimes he would take people to universities or specific houses or in one case a lady wanted to go to her aged care facility. Then he finds his car and awakens. According to the books he helps people who have passed over to find where they are supposed to go.

One time he couldn't find his car and as a result he couldn't wake up. This was a horrid experience, he kept thinking he was awake but he wasn't, so he'd try again. When he did finally awaken, he felt quite nauseous for the rest of the day. He found out later this is known as sleep paralysis.

His astral body went to a bed room of a woman. He went close to the bed and it was Roxy. He knelt down beside the sleeping body and bent over to kiss her but she startled and rolled over. He stood up then bent down to kiss her gently on the cheek; slowly and gently he glided back to his body.

Next morning, he felt drained when he had to go for his run and swim. His mind was filled with anticipation of the conversations with Jesse It had him speculating the coming events of her catering and how that would take place and now this new revelation of his dream and desiring to kiss her.

After breakfast he drove to the studio, set himself up and prepared himself for his first round of clients. Jesse arrived; was chipper and ready for a good days recording. He had received the main tape of the performance on Saturday night and he was ready to edit and reproduce them for sale on their web page.

They swapped early morning chit chat and both went to work. The first of Jai's clients arrived and he place him in the monitoring room. He started his computerised deep therapy session with his male client to assist him with his smoking which was serious and would probably kill him. This was his clients second week. Jai was very impressed as his stress levels had dropped and he was now down to 10 per day. This was a huge improvement from a minimum of forty per day.

One of Jai's clients had taken the same course about eighteen months prior and he met up with him at a social. Since he saw him last, he had lost his job, moved house, and he doesn't smoke at all. Jai was most apologetic. No said his client. It was the best thing that ever happened. I have a new job; I've taken a pay cut and I have so much more time with my family and I've never been happier. He took Jai's hand and shook it with both of his, "I really want to thank you." Jai was impressed and uses this reaction as a promotion spiff for his new clients.

This client's session took 50 minutes and he quietly left booking his last treatment for Friday. Jai's second client was running on time and due on the hour, which gave Jai sufficient time to clean up the monitoring room in preparation.

Once this client was settled, he joined him for his session and basically did the same as he had done for his previous client. This client was a beginner but the sessions were the same.

Jai then proceeded with his last client for the morning and decided to take a break; a deliberate break. His next client was at one in the afternoon so he had an hour. Jesse was busily working away with the screening of the DVD. He edited the lighting, the sound, he was on a roll in his own soundproof booth.

Jai tapped on the glass pointed to his watch, indicating time for a break. Jesse responded in a few minutes. Jesse finished up and came out for his prepared lunch. There is a kitchen with all conveniences for lunch and dinner. Jai often stayed over so he would use the oven and stove cooktop for his meals. He enjoyed cooking and always has a full fridge.

As they both quietly go about preparing their individual meals Jai very coolly slid into the conversation and asks if Jesse has tried out the new café. The conversation criss-crosses then he politely dropped the bomb shell that Roxy, the blonde he bumped into on the street and had that vision, is the owner.

Jesse shook his head and snidely remarked "do you have a death wish?" he shook his head "this woman is out of reach to you," he paused. Jai was stunned at his remark and was about to interrupt when Jesse interceded again. "You have nothing."

"Well there is more" Jai then began to inform him of his astral adventure last night. There was silence and Jai was hoping for an inspirational answer, but there was nothing. Jai started speaking in circles trying to find justification or validation for all of this. He was sure there had to be a reason, because he was twisted and anxious inside and he's never like that.

Jai's next client would arrive soon so they started to tidy up and return to work. His next client was having a life regression. This session is long and enduring and Jai needed to be calm and together. He invited his client into his sound proof room specially designed for this procedure. Due to the length of these sessions complete silence from the exterior world has proven to be very successful. This way Jai has complete control of the session. All phones, doors and all forms of interruptions are restricted unless emergency.

Comfort for both client and practitioner are a must to attain the highest success. The client filled out a questionnaire so Jai can determine what the client is searching for and from this he will base his questions. Concentration and focus for the entire period is essential, and this is one of the reasons Jai works out; it maintains his stamina, however today he will have to maintain extra precautions against the tiredness during the long session.

Jai set his watch for a warning buzzer to maintain control of the session. By the time all the paper work is completed and formalities are done the time is about 1.30 pm. Jai's has to place the patient in to a tranced state where they can respond verbally; this takes about 20 minutes; then from there he is able to take the client even deeper into their past, then eventually into their past life. The room must be warm and the seat must almost feel like a cloud creating a sense of floating.

The first session is always the most difficult for it is the training of the subconscious to travel under someone's else's' instructions. Maintaining security and safety is vital at all times. The subconscious of the client must feel secure at all times so it will trust you to ask the questions. If a client cannot be hypnotised, this is where the challenge arises. The subconscious does not feel safe and creates caution trying to control the situation.

This is where the soft background music has proven successful. Jai will encourage the client to focus on the music while he talks to the subconscious and allow them to travel at their own pace.

This client was comfortable and the session was a success. She achieved a brilliant experience with all the information she needed. She would like another. Jai arranged another session in about one month.

It had proven to be a long day and when it all finished Jai went to search for Jesse but he was gone. He went to his office and filed all the paper work, placed the tape of the session in the library, cleaned up the studio then locked the doors and decided to go for another coffee at the "waterside café" on the way home. He was hoping to catch another glimpse of the woman who was haunting him. He went in but only Jason was working, so he bought his drink and went home. At least now he knows she doesn't work on Mondays.

Over the next few weeks Jai concentrated on things that mattered. He wanted to arrange another performance at the same venue but may be this time he would create it for a little longer period. He was contemplating a Saturday or Sunday session.

To achieve that, he had to have vital information that his audience would want to listen to. As is the way with paths if you create from inside all the formations fall into place and come to you. Without even knowing it all the components of the future successful event was falling into place and coming to him.

His library had official proof of his teachings and he started on the path of teaching how to 'watch your step.' To do that he had to revise authentic history, philosophy and his tapes evidence and have them all comply. This seminar will be controversial and will rock traditionalist and he may not get a huge gathering, but those who come will enjoy his new philosophies.

He contacted Alex and asked him to start making arrangements for him to look over, prepare options of venues, cost, and food availability. He stated he wanted the Waterside to cater as Jason was a friend, he might give us a discount, plus they also offer the option of organic and healthy food.

He had to contact his accountant to make sure there was sufficient funds available for this new venture along with-its availability. The energy was moving and becoming vibrant again. It had been a bit of a lull since the last seminar and it was time to pick things up again

CHAPTER 4

MEETING ROXY

Jason had been a long-time friend with Jai so for their relationship to continue on that path was a natural. Jason had altered his place of employment and Jai like many of Jason's customers would follow due to his excellent service and friendship.

However, what wasn't on the agenda was Roxy. This woman was getting more and more under his skin every time he saw her. There was a very strong magnetic force drawing him to her; was it their common interest in past life occurrences? Finding someone who knew what he was expressing and believing in, this would create an attraction.

Roxy asked about his upcoming event and what he proposed to speak about. This initiation opened the flood gates to ongoing stimulating conversations. Einstein quoted that the most sensual emotion to experience is an intelligent conversation. His quote would be the foreplay to many a stimulating afternoon in her café.

They would compare opinions and he discovered she had a more feminine approach to his teachings. She opened his mind to the wants and needs of women. She pointed out that he was basically the instrument of the dimension of the time and the people who came to his seminars were searching for something better. If he used his sexuality properly, he could sensually transport both women and men to a new understanding of the true bonds of soul partnerships and diminish the separation theory.

Roxy accentuated that the immense separation we feel as humans is our division within ourselves, not with a god and not with each other.

She further divulged that she had been studying the narcissist syndrome and was surprised to almost see it everywhere she looked. The narcissistic male supremists believe they can control and do everything and as such, requisites that everything be subservient to them. Displaying exhilarating passion, she continued, "Now is the time for all the subservient, especially women, to stand up and basically say, "well you've shown us what you can do and this is the result; sorry boys it's not good enough.

Your job now is to reach into the women with all the right philosophies, idioms and colloquialisms and give them the garments they need to get out from under the oppression and rise above man with a new found love and respect for themselves. That will empower them to be more."

Roxy was passionate about this new empowering love being strong enough to not only raise them to new heights but give them the self-empowerment they need to be able to say; "this is what I want. We, as unison; not separated and together and equal out of the love we have for us. We can create a far better future for everyone."

Women have to be strong enough to say "you want to play with me you have to raise your standards and change your game. Your stuff, your money, your egoistic attitude, is not what will make us happy, our love together will. You have divided us as humans. You have enslaved, and victimised and that creates horrific bleeding, pain, hurt and suffering thus, creating more. We are at that stage where we cannot recognise our soul anymore and we'll accept anything that looks like acceptance. We keep doing whatever it takes to bury and hide, using the very thing that is hurting us; money, wealth, fortresses, food, sex addictions, wars the lot.

The world around us is informing us of what we have done and what we are constantly doing. It is demonstrating this incessant implosion of emotions we insist on using to prevent us from having what we really want. To let go of the pain we have to first accept it and own it, acknowledge that we created it, then let it go.

Until you are re-joined as one with your true consciousness and mind you will never feel whole. That's why when you start loving yourself the way your soul would love you; you then start attracting all the amazing stuff to you. It all comes to you; it lands in your lap."

She grabbed his hand and kept speaking enthusiastically with an admiring smile on her face she lowered her voice and she continued "When you see an aged couple holding hands and walking together, it is the hand holding that tells you they have found their soul mate, that is their soul speaking." Realising she was holding his hand she quickly released it back onto the table.

This material gave Jai an entirely new format to work with. Adding this to his Watch Your Step format gave him a complete half day seminar.

He was becoming extremely keen with this new format that he enjoyed running copies past Roxy for editing. He has never done this before. He was practicing what she was teaching. The unison of male and female creates higher empowerment for both. Being a sole parent for over twenty years this "joining forces" with someone on a project so important to him was an entirely new process.

He was more than enjoying the company. He kept convincing himself that it was business and she was just a friend, but the enjoyment was on higher levels of satiation. The seminar was getting closer and his work was coming to a finish and he didn't really want that to occur.

Less than a week to go. The conference was important for it was the first half day seminar he had attempted. He needed the audience to participate and interact with him at the same time not taking over. He had to anticipate questions and the retribution from those who disapproved of his controversial ideas.

He asked Roxy if she'd be a guest speaker to break the monotony but she refused, saying he was simply trying to overcome his nerves. If he felt it was monotonous, alter it, until he was happy with what will make it more inspiring.

Her advice, although true, really wasn't warranted; he felt really pleased with the content of his oration. His only reserve was when Roxy shared her information, she displayed an intense passion and her hands would express the word as if she was playing a Spanish guitar. Her fingers would move and caress the air around her as the words came out of her mouth expressing what her hands were saying. It was like listening to music. He didn't possess that flare or passion.

He loved what he was doing and loved interacting with the audiences but genuinely lacked her exaggerated sparkle and expression of her words to personify the language.

Jai jestingly commented on her talking with her hands and she quickly stopped doing it hiding them. He gently grabbed them and apologised for he loved it. She commented that it was her soul speaking.

Then laughed as she added, "sometimes they are a real chatter box."

She wished him luck for his big night as she prepared for hers. They were being hired as the caterers. In previous shows he allowed twenty minutes intervals but Roxy asked for two intervals of half an hour. There would be approximately 700 people and they would need the time. This was agreed upon; now she needed a good menu to accommodate 700 people.

Easily accessible fast food both hot and cold; and sufficient experienced staff to handle the crowd:

She also needed staff to stay behind and take care of the café, so this was a huge undertaking for her. She would send Jason and six crew to the venue, while she and four crew would maintain the café. She hired a catering truck to transport the food to the venue and trusted Jason completely. He convinced her he was capable of handling it. He had done functions before and was quite experienced. If he succeeded this time maybe they could open up to more outside functions.

This was his dream to promote this kiosk to be the best in the bay. This was his opportunity to prove it.

CHAPTER 5

HALF DAY SEMINAR

WATCH YOUR STEP

As usual the crowd jump to their feet and applauded loudly as Jai waltzed on to the highly lit stage waving and greeting his over excited audience. The Emcee had given him a vibrant intro and prepared the audience for a spectacular day.

"Thank you, thank you, thank you," he exclaimed in a higher voice than usual. "Wow this is going to be a big day so let's get started.

We're going to do an hour and a bit, then we'll give you half an hour for a quick break; then we'll do another hour and a bit, then another half hour break, then to the finale. As Roger the emcee stated there are books tapes and video are on sale during the entire performance in the foyer and today, we have 30% of everything.

Let get started; As Roger stated my name is Jai Tagore, I run a hypnotherapy studio at the Bay with a brilliant colleague. We specialise in past life regressions and life between life sessions but I also specialise in what we call "The Reincarnation Continuum." Reincarnation is not where we pop in and have a life here and there to simply experience something new, unfortunately there are laws of the universe that prevent that, and all beings have to exist by them.

Our universe like all others reacts magnetically and the basic fundamental of 'like attract like and opposites repel' do dictates the rules of our very existence. Understanding how these rules affect our lives is The Reincarnation Continuum. The beauty of understanding the continuum is, by utilising the same rules, we are able to manipulate the rules to our advantage, alter our lives and manifest more exciting futures, and that's what we are her for today.

Karma, Law of attachment, and everybody's favourite Law of attraction, these are our instruments. Always treat them with respect for the way your treat them is they response you will receive. The next rule is; **nothing exists until we create it.** Some of you may find that statement a bit confusing but it is a fact, and we create new emotions every second of every day by reacting.

What you may not know is that the law of Karma then translates that emotion into binary in your DNA instantly and that very emotion now personifies you. You now perform as that emotion. How? The DNA converts that emotion into binary information and it becomes an attachment in every cell in your body. The fractal of that emotion which is similar to one-bathroom tile. It has all the information of the entire tiled bathroom and from there the Law of Attraction complies and matches your binary to every matrix binary in the universe for you to experience.

The people, the places, your careers, your health, wealth and happiness are all determined from that one emotional creative thought. The equation is simple; you react and create, karma personifies it; the law of attachment connects it and the Law of attraction magnifies every emotion similar to it for you to experience. Now if you realise this is how it works and recognise that everything around you now is simply feedback as opposed to something to react to, you now have the power to alter your future situations.

Let get started; 'Watch your step' is a duplicitous name for this seminar but it doesn't mean step ladder or staircase it means become an objective observer of your own life. Yes, that means a non-participant and then a responder.

The argument that debates this philosophy is we are meant to live our lives now so why are we here?

The answer to that is simply; You haven't been living your lives you have been reacting to them. You have existed for over 70 million years as humans and this is where you have ended up. Are you happy with the results? Now it's time to step back and have a really good look at what you have and haven't accomplished. It's time to pay the ferry man so to speak. It's time to assess our situation and renegotiate some of our behavioural patterns.

There's beautiful woman whom I collaborate with and her opinion of how things have turned out and my opinion of what is happening in the world could not be further apart.

She speaks passionately about the lack of equality for lessor beings and how man rules the roost. Now from a male perspective, I will defend our gender and state that we have progressed and changed the world to a faster more proficient place to live. Her argument is due to our brilliant consciousness that would have occurred anyway." He throws his hands up in the air.

"Her challenge to this is very simple; "if we keep continuing on this path, we'll *proficient* ourselves right out of existence." There is sporadic applause around the audience.

"Thank you for that intermittent applause I'll let her know you agreed" he laughs.

"The entire argument here is what we see in our exterior world is what we created.

We are not victims of our past, we simply keep creating victimising circumstances due to our own perceptions. At the moment, we are not people who can learn from our past. We refuse to acknowledge that we created it and are continuing to create it. As a result, due to those two incorrect perceptions we have absolutely no idea how to either stop or prevent it.

We have the uncanny ability to be able to separate ourselves from those of our past, and we are trying to fix up the now with even less competence. Our governments and politicians and top business men have no idea how to resolve the situation and maybe my friend is right we will proficient ourselves into extinction.

What we don't want to accept is, we created all these tsunamis. They are pulling us along and unless we make genuine changes to our thinking patterns, this engulfing force will keep reacting to our creations and continue forward finally dictating the demise or our extinction. The past, the present and the future are connected to us.

We were there, are there and will be there and we are responsible. We created the cause and effect that has bought us to this moment, and the future moments.

Okay give me a minute, I'm coming down there, among you."

Jai started leaving the stage down the side stairs to stand directly in front of his audience. "This way I can see your reactions and you can interact with me more." As he started pacing up and down in front of them, he began speaking again. The DVD recording had him placed on the screen at the back of the stage so everyone could still see him.

"Okay now" he continued. "How do we know which part of history we participated in and which part are we responsible for? There are several ways now to find out about your past lives, one is of course hypnosis with past life regression. This can take several attempts and a considerable amount of money, or two; you learn to read your environment.

You can learn how to become an objective observer. You start interpreting your entire environment. You created the entire thing now discover what you created. That last statement will eventually alter to; you start interpreting the things that are happening *for* you as opposed to, *to* you.

Why would that sentence alter? It alters because everything around you is occurring as feedback information for you to interpret; It's the data and you are the computer. Now you have the choice. You can continue reacting to it thus creating more of the same or, you can read it and respond to it and make a difference. Every single person place and thing around you is there to specifically inform you of your location in your rhythm of life."

Jai starts climbing the aisle stairways within the audience. The video camera still has him in their sights and those in the front and the back are still able to watch him on the screen.

"This is the most important information I can share with you at the moment. Why? Take this home with you.

Nothing is done here on earth to harm you; everything is done to assist you. Nothing is done to harm you; everything is done out of love for you; by you.

Now some of you may say 'well you haven't met my ex-wife or ex-husband' and you are right I haven't met yours but I do have a couple of my own and yes, our break ups weren't the happiest period of my life.

What if I was to tell you that you deliberately asked them to participate in your life and that your breaking up was an essential component of your future path? If it wasn't for them you would not be at this place in your life."

Jai starts bounding down the stairs to the front of the audience again. "Now some of you may be saying, now you want me to give them credit for my success?" The audience laughs. "Well in a way yes.

Whatever the energy was that motivated you to move, is the energy you needed to start your new path. You would not have received that from anyone else. To be able to rise above the situation you were in, you needed to be put in a position of huge discomfort so you could move. That was your choice" he pauses and take a breath.

"You and your ex-partner devised a plan to push your buttons to the level where you would gain that motivated stance to move; congratulations; success, you did it. Now here's the bonus; if you are able to accept that you allowed that experience to take place so you could advance to a more proficient level; what you and your ex are doing is eradicating the very victimising essentials that has been preventing both of you from progressing further.

In this one simple act you have become an objective observer of your own life. No judgement or reaction, you recognised that, that person came here the same as you did. You gave that person what they needed to proceed further as well.

Without your assistance, be it philandering, jealousy, abuse, you name it; you both decided that this experience would be carried out this way. Now that it is done, leave it alone. By leaving it alone you are allowing, respecting, creating equality, self-love, self-respect and most of all self-empowerment. You are literally walking away from your own power of victimisation. Once you open that door it produces a cacophony of chaos in every area of your life. Every cell of your body emanates it and every component of your existence experiences it.

From this one experience you are able to deduce the cause and effect of your life and how past influences determine your life now and your future.

That was a simple exercise, any questions?

Good now quickly turn to person beside you if you don't know them introduce yourself and quickly explain it,"

As the audience stirs, Jai scampers to the other side of the venue and starts walking up the second stairway preparing himself for his next communication.

"Okay everybody happy?" Jai notices that a high percentage of his audience are female so he starts confidently having a bit of fun with some smiles, flirting and winking. He swiftly diverts from lecturer to entertainer.

"So if you are able to decipher the challenges that have defined you as a person; break them down and analysis them, from this new perspective you will come to the decision that everyone in your life for one purpose or another came to help you not hurt you; how do you think that is going to make you feel about the world.

Your personal world is now not as tragic because everything that was done to you was actually done for you; so, your world is really not so bad after all, is it? In fact, you could say it's almost perfect.

Well you could, but that doesn't determine how these actions and all the actions of the past have bought you to this point. With this new information you are able to renegotiate this action because you can recall your participation in it. You remember the actions that took place.

The past actions in this life time, you can generalise them and say well I'm here because of them but that really doesn't give you the material you need to understand how your past has bought you to this point."

He slowly starts descending the stairs to return to the front of the audience.

"What if I were to tell you that all actions around you are feedback informing you of your past life behaviours and by watching them and reading them you are able to predict your future path?"

He starts smirking.

"Ooh now we're doing the spooky stuff." He giggles and makes some suggestive faces to the audience and they respond.

"Let's start small. You and your friends decide to have a coffee. This action is something that occurs every day. People are doing it everywhere." He throws his arms up as if to query.

"Technical stuff first; you are all there because in your past you all made an emotional judgement and created an emotion. That emotion, that didn't exist until you all created it, is now defining you all as a people; the law of attraction draws you to this time in existence to expose that same emotion in this life time. To explain further with a simple example.

In your past life you were Indian like me; you hated the white man and you constantly made harsh statements that they were philandering, jealous, envious, drunkards. The emotional intent, in this case prejudice and hatred, behind the words is defining each word for you to experience. In this life time, due to your innocent opinion, you actually created that future path of the English man for yourself to experience.

I can define that even further if you like; let's say you are about thirty when you passed this judgement and you say it for twelve years. There is a very good possibility that at the same age of thirty in this existence for twelve years you will be that debaucherously drunken English person; that's how precise this action is. Through your creative reaction to your emotion of hatred, you write your future script. This used to be called Exacting Karma or history repeating itself. The truth is, karma actually created you by following your instructions word for word.

Am I making that up? No. Past life regression hypnotherapy discoveries have uncovered these coincidences." Jai points to himself with both hands in a humorous manner he continues "In the past I was the brilliant Englishman who judged Polynesian Indians, if they existed then," he and the audience laughs. "As a friend says I probably judged all colours, so in this life I simply morphed them. The point is you weren't always who you are now.

From that perspective you are now able to recognise that a past life influence has bought you to this point

Everything in this life is affected in this way. You go to a cafe with your friends. You all made a judgement call in the past through an emotion. That emotion is drawing you all to the coffee table, the café, and the place and town where the café is situated. This is the tsunami you created in your past life; it is pulling you all together again," he pauses and in a joking voice " and you thought it was the coffee. Now this is the fundamental point; why are you all there?

Is it a gossip group; is it a backstabbing group; or are you a group there to support and help not only the group but others as well. The very judgemental acts taking place at that table are depicting the very same judgements from your past, only now you are on the receiving end, the deciphering end.

So, if that is what happened in your past and it is determining your present, what is this little soiree depicting for your future path? Answer; every thought word and action taking place at that table; exercise complete." He pauses to let them think.

"You, by observing this get together have deciphered how you arrived there. The mood, the imbalance, the nastiness, or the loveliness. Through each of these emotions as you speak, every word that comes out of your mouth defines you and mirrors them; nasty, sweet, malice, objective, argumentative; your reaction to your friends will predict your future path. Got it; understand it; any questions? Good now share that with your neighbour."

As the audience muttered between themselves, Jai makes his way back to the stage to the dais to check his computer for power point.

He was going to use it but there is only one screen so he decided to leave it.

"Okay how we going? Is everybody still with me? Are there any complications?" he watches audience reactions "Great we are on time, so after this next section we'll be letting you have you first half hour break. There is hot and cold food and drinks available.

Let's begin. From the exercises so far, you are able to depict your now life from your past experiences in this life. You are able to determine the past life actions that have bought you to this point and from that action you can now determine your future path."

Jai changes the screens with the Buddhist quote;

LIFE IS AN ECHO:
WHAT YOU SEND OUT COMES BACK:
WHAT YOU SOW YOU REAP:
WHAT YOU GIVE YOU GET:
WHAT YOU SEE IN OTHERS,
EXISTS IN YOU:

"Read the quote and many will believe it refers to this life only. Stretch your imagination to recognise that this quote refers to all your past lives as well. This is law of attraction and the extent that this law will go to, to magnetise the emotionally personified people, and the places, to you. Every single one of you was magnetically drawn to the coffee table because of that emotion you created from your past judgement, either earlier in this life or a past life

Do you understand that?" There are nods but some shakes as well. "Okay for those who are having difficulty. He questions where they are having difficulty. A couple respond, and he answers, "creating from the nothing-ness?" he queries. He pauses and breathe in, "okay." Jai collects his thoughts.

"You watch Star Wars. You do not like Darth Vader.

However, before Star Wars that emotion didn't exit. You didn't create that emotion until you saw Darth Vader. Now Darth Vader is simply Darth Vader, he's nothing he doesn't exist, but the emotion within you is real, you created it. Until you created it, it didn't exist. Darth Vader is not responsible for your creation; you are and from that emotion karma will personify it within you; law of attachment will place it in every single gene and the law of attraction will bring your more. And it did how many more did we get. Six, seven? Understand now, good?

Back to the coffee shop. Every one of you echoed each other and then they mirrored your future path. The emotion for all of you is the same. You all personify that one emotion. Gossip, backstabbing, malice; one of these emotions will dictate the get together. Now the reason I say this is to support my evidence by a master who existed thousands of years ago. If you wanted to learn this information then you had to join a temple.

Well not all of us are inclined that way and if you're a woman you were not allowed to enter.

"Hey don't look at me like that" referring to some women in the front row. "I didn't make the rules" they laugh, "Hey you think that's bad; some guys really didn't like you girls at all;" still conversing with the ladies in the front row.

Montaigne for example is quoted saying" he paused so he got their attention then continued, *"Pleasure with women is like shitting in a basket so you can dump it on your head afterwards." He laughs as he says it in disbelief shaking his head.*

"I mean what did you girls do to piss him off?"

He paused a while as they laughed; he raises his hands up in a defensive motion. "Sorry but, hey I don't feel that way, I quite enjoy your company," he catches his breath as he continues shaking his head while still smiling. "We'll be doing more on that this afternoon but let's get back to this or you'll never get your break.

Okay, where were we? Right you're an echo of your past life. To clarify that you are a miniscule light surrounded by a perfectly shaped astral body that never ages. Your physical body however, is the outcome of all your past histories; your evolution. Your illness, your eyes, your height, your weight problems, all culminations of emotional judgements from your past; then your auric field is a culmination of binary codes depicting your past life history in a magnetic field that attracts more of your past to you. You echo or mirror your past history. All that history is attached to emotions, and your emotions start in your head with a perception. You created them from your head/your perception, then your mouth.

Once your mouth speaks and determines what it wants created, karma personifies the words and the law of attachment binds them to every cell in your body. When you feel the anger or you feel the injustice or you feel the lack of control; all those emotional feelings are translated in the blink of an eye. When you love, hate, enjoy another's company, that reaction is the binary information in your auric fields that is explaining your emotional disturbance. That information is impelled inwards toward your body.

The Prophet

Your past life history duplicates you in your appearance, your attitude to material needs, and those appearances magnetically draws you to your family, friends, enemies, lovers and work mates at specific times; and let's not forget to add pets as well. In many cases I see where a child gets a pet, they cannot take care of, the parent will take care of it. The pet was meant to be with the parent and it had to take the long way round to acquire it.

This happens with relationships also, and again more on this this afternoon.

Your entire past life history is within you and around you. How do you recognise it in other areas of your life?

What shows do you enjoy on television, movies, football or other sport. What type of books do you read that includes magazines; what type of activities do you enjoy? Every particle of your existence is in connection with your pastlife. Every action is informing you of where you came from and where you are going.

Now you have to compare that with what you are being shown in history. What are you interested in? Do you like Merlin and the round table of King Arthur? Are you interested in the crusades? Here's one, are you interested in religion? There's a history in itself. What type of work do you do? Is it creative or are you a slave to your position and the place and you only work for the money? All these important details in your life are telling you the cause and effect of your past life.

Your wear your garment of history. Then you attract to you all the things around you to inform you of the garment you are wearing. Do you understand that?" He was surrounded by nods and agreement; "okay then do a quick session with your neighbour."

He waits for about half a minute, "Now if you have weight problems, you have anxiety, your smoke heavily, come and see me I can fix that, but all these issues are vital information about your entire life. They are telling you something is out of control. We do not die; our bodies do but we don't; we keep returning because the magnetic force of the law of attraction draws us back to continue our journey.

If you were a murderer, to balance your journey you will become the victim." He pauses for a moment emphasising, "by choice." He pauses again. "You choose to heal you, so you opt for the existence to heal you and balance you. The question is how did you get caught up in the situation of murder in the first place? A perceptional judgment," he pauses again. "Through your perception of what is occurring, you judge from that view point.

"An inadvertent act of judgement against a murderer centuries ago; let's say the path of the murder is five steps or five lifetimes; the first step is the act of judgement. You critique, you accuse, you advise, you gossip, you back stab; these actions will be added to you next existence and your next and your next until you are the murderer followed by the victim, then the path will be finished.

The existences may evolve like one may be where you learn to hunt for food so now you have the weapon, the next one you kill people and the next one you are the victim.

This is what I mean by tsunami; because of this minor judgement for justice, not realising that the victim it is at the final sequence of events; you become part of entirely new ongoing synopsis starting at the beginning.

Clearer explanation; the victim is at the top of the ladder finished done. You have to start at the bottom and go through each rung till you reach the top, you have no choice. This is the ongoing synopsis of the reincarnation continuum. This is life and history repeating itself in an ongoing circle like the inside of a conchae shell.

This is not a direct path outline, but what is definite is once you judge, you go on that path until it is done. This is the garment you are wearing and from the moment of your judgement the law of attraction will bring to you all the intricate components to ensure you achieve your full journey. Now in each existence more murders will be displayed around you informing you of the path you are on and the magnetic force will have you judging them again to maintain the path; this is the law of attraction constantly informing you of the path you are on. This is the linear procession.

One important issue to recognise is once the murder has been completed for the victim it is over, it is done, and he has now resolved the hate issues caused by his initial judgement centuries ago. For the perpetrator he will endure one more existence by being the victim in his next life. So, in truth the entire scenario is finished, completed.

Because you or others judge, then the continuum will keep occurring; the judges, juries, they are all accounted for and they have been placed there through their judgement and yes, they will follow suit in one form or another, but you really don't have to.

By allowing the situation to flow without your input, you will not succumb to the victimising path. By doing this you are releasing your judgement, your control, and you are creating a better path for you to walk.

What happens then is; situations of murder, slaying, don't appear in your views anymore. That then means if you were on that path you have now altered it. Same goes for the coffee shop; in front of you is the group of people who are telling you the path you are on.

If you don't want to continue on the path of the people you are backstabbing, in other words if you choose to no longer be victim to your past life emotions and have others betray you, walk away and alter your path.

Once you do that, they won't call you any more for their coffee club, why because you have created a better path; your choice. Your outside binary has been altered.

Okay I'm being told to wind up; this brings us to your first break. You have half an hour so we'll meet here at quarter to okay, enjoy your break."

CHAPTER 6

FIRST BREAK

This seminar was having a good reaction; however, the next two parts were crucial to the climax and success of his new book which was released one month ago. Introducing a book at the seminar is a gimmick promoted by Alex to increase sales. It gives promotion of sales a boost and a kick start to more sales from his web page because Jesse adds in the photographs from the seminar. Alex always takes advantage of the breaks by promoting all Jai's books and tapes.

Meanwhile Jai changes his shirt again in to a cooler one of pure cotton which will hang softly over his firm fitting jeans. He goes over his notes and the appendages. He rechecks the flow for the final section for his talks must have impact. He sits, he breathes, has a quick sandwich and drink while he collects his thoughts.

"Hi and we're back; all refreshed and ready for round two? The objective of this part of the seminar is to waken the soul. Now I know many of the guys aren't really into this but there are two really good reasons why you need to alter your perspective. The women and you are here because you are looking for more in your life.

By adjusting to higher level of thinking you open an entirely new door to what you are used to. Yes, I'm talking the weird eerie stuff. Yeah, some guys are into it but many would rather watch the football.

Sure, the wife loves a bit of footy too but they are here because there is more to life than what you are offering; same goes for you; you can have more without paying out elaborate amounts of money.

Two; the women have the key to the entire success to all the rest of existence. If you want the best of the best, she is the key to acquiring it. I'm not trying to get extra brownie points here with the women even though that's not a bad sale pitch; the very breath of women is the key to all our future success but here's the problem; they... don't... know it... either; sorry girls.

As I said earlier when you look at the situation of the world, we as men are simply moving with the tide and that's the way it is. We've had the philosophers, the teachers, the gurus and nothing has changed. This is simply the way it is. There will always be wars; genocide, poor, and struggle that's just how it is. You have to work around it.

According to the women of the world, male dominance has ruled the roost for over 70000 years and this is all we have to offer, and there is no light at the end of the tunnel. What's more we plan on expanding out into space and doing more of it.

Now the women are standing up and saying after all these years of you having it all your way and this is all you have to offer. This is it? Well it's not good enough.

So, what if instead of saying, that's the way it is, what if we asked, what isn't it?

To touch basics. I'm not going to do the god thing here but we do have to realise we are not separated from the godness thing. It's like the fish in the ocean. The ocean depends on the fish and the fish depends on everything in the ocean. Everything in the ocean is dependent on each other and vice versa. If the fish doesn't believe in the ocean the ocean isn't going to dry up or freeze over because of the belief of the fish. It will go on giving the fish everything it needs to survive. Same with everything around us. It will exist whether you believe or not. Like the ocean you cannot survive without it.

So, if we are not separated, why are we creating this duality and separation? What are we separated from? What is the dividing force separating us: because we are divided? There is segregation, racism, sexism, all issues of being separated from others. Our world is telling us we are separated; but from what?

If we look back over our history our story is not a pretty one. Under the guise of strength and force which created the wars, battles, feuds, there is a constant path of devastation and destruction dating back hundreds of thousands of years. That is the top plane.

Under that superior dominance plane is another plane of the subservience. Women, children, coloured people, natives, animals, land, forests oceans all suffering under the regime of hatred, anger, abuse, dominance and separation. This is the gift from the self-important dominant emotion.

After centuries of anger, pain and loss we actually manifest more of the same pain by reacting to it for us to return to. We have to find the honest resolution to alter our future paths.

This path of love has been presented before and every time it has surfaced it has been crushed by the same egocentric attitude of dominance to prevent lack of control.

Because of this, when we try to create equality of all things, we can only use the tools of the domineering sector to achieve it; you have to rise to the level of the domineering sector and fight them on their terms. This action of the fight actually empowers the domineering faction and the fight creates more disorder and the cycle continues.

Like all narcissistic relationships, you will rise to the level of the narcissist this dominant force will force you into subservience again but it will add extra kilos of hatred with it so you cannot return, then they will return to the old scenario.

Einstein says '**Insanity**; doing the same thing over and over again and expecting different results. You cannot solve a problem using the same mind that created it.'

Ladies you have a huge task ahead of you if you choose to take the mission. What makes the universe absolutely perfect is its unison, its oneness, and that is unconditional love. The God of all things loves unconditionally now you have to do the same. How do you do that? You have to create the complete mind frame of unconditional love and acceptance within you first, which will liberate you from your subservience of the victimising regime you are now imprisoned in.

By releasing all your past life griefs and realising all is perfect, you break the imprisoning binds of your past, now you can create love and from that new perception and create an amazing future.

To visualise what I'm talking about you have to imagine all the subservient beings on the lowest plane, then man with his materialistic values on the next level domineering and bullying all other beings into slavery. To be redeemed you," as he point around the room to the women, " women, don't raise yourself to the fighting level of man for equality for when you do this you do become equal to man; You are using the same tools as man and thus that action will define you as male. Ladies you have to raise yourself above both levels; the subservient level of the serving victimising female and the domineering male There is only one way to do this; through the unison of unconditional self-love. To do that you have to relinquish all victimising action.

One, you have to recognise them around you and two, you have to recognise them within you.

Ladies also, you have to realise that eventually they too cannot do this on their own. It is only when you are reconnected to your soul mate completely, then both of you are able to acquire this higher level of consciousness and received all the universe has to offer.

NO MORE SLAVERY. EQUALITY FOR ALL.

Our plan here today is to assist you in realising that the basic thing that is missing in our dimension today is our personal self-love. We haven't been separated from our god we have been separated from us.

WE COMPLETE US.

We are capable of creating anything we want and when we create outside of us, we attain what we have already created to date. When you learn to create for your inner self from the godness within you, this is the very creative wholeness of the universe and you attain all the universe can offer.

We have found that we only have one soul mate, and many times through each existence we try to find them but due to our past life judgements and abuse, we get separated from them; very few people today find their true soul mate. However, you can tell people who have found their soul mates; they hold hands, well into their old age and never let them go.

HOLDING HANDS! Are you kidding me?" There is giggling in the audience. "No seriously; when you see and aged couple holding hands when they are walking together, they are soul mates. I'm not saying when one's arms are linked with each other; that's an English custom dating back centuries to assist women across potholes or try to walk in their fine heeled shoes. The hands are the vortex to the soul. When they are continually holding hands, their souls are connecting. It's all very sexy." He makes a suggestive face to the audience then there is a giggle throughout the venue.

"See this part of the hands" he holds his hands up and point to the centre of the palm; and then he circles his finger into the very centre of the palm, "this is a very sexy meridian. In Karma sutra, Kundalini, many of the ancient rituals, this part of the hand was used to arouse the female to a more erotic level," he giggles as he continues, "so both people holding hands are very sexy." He gives a wink and continues.

"I'm getting some funny looks from the front row here; to clarify, no they are not having soul sex" he laughs as he continues" but the souls are connecting. When you talk to these people, they say they cannot go anywhere without their partner and when they do hold each other hands is automatic, they don't even know they are doing it. In the movie Sleepless in Seattle Tom Hanks says, he simply took her hand and he knew. Her mother speaks of how when holding her father's hand, she couldn't tell where her hand stopped and his began. That's connection; that's the oneness.

"Aww!" Jai says in jest. The crowd responds. "That's sexy. Another development in talking with these people; they didn't have the drama and traumas of everyday people. They had a happy marriage, loving children, great grandchildren. They both had great jobs, their health is great, this is the second or third home and they cannot complain about life they were always happy.

They actually live Buddha's quote of living in the world but not of the world. It's like watching happy days on television.

So, what makes their life so different from the average Joe? 'Their personal soul connection. They are not victim to their outside world of victimisation' It brings all the good things to them. They never search.

To be able to reach this level of love and connection you have to be able to *allow* all the history of your past. Then you have to want to rise above the planes that you now exist on.

To completely understand that, you have to take all the lessons from this morning; the acknowledgement that all is perfect; the knowing that nothing is here to hurt you and release all of it deliberately choose not to be a victim to them; then release all forms of judgement from future disastrous calamities, then start walking your future path now.

You want to be with in love the ultimate love of all your lives; your soul mate; be in complete love with you first. That's round one. Be completely in love with you first. The reason you are uncomfortable with the world is because you are uncomfortable with you. Change your attitude to you and the world will change its attitude to you.

In the fifties and sixties after the war women wanted to stay in the work force. However, in the male dominant structure this would cut into their profit margins; so, women worked at half the pay salary as men even though they worked just as hard or harder. In a lot of cases they were given the tedious difficult jobs and the men climbed the ladder of success. Guys I'm not putting you down but this is what we did to them. However, this is our nah nah moment.

Throughout history, both men and women have participated in this dominant narcissistic emotional world at one time or another.

The soul is non-gender so to experience all aspects of these lives, it wears all garments.

It is not a matter of gender. We are desperately reacting to a pain, so we will use whatever tool is available to us to fight back. One life time we may use the slavery of the female, then the dominance of male, the abuse of same sex, the denigration of war poverty all the pains to express our concern, at the same time revealing to ourselves that we are using the very tools that are creating it, while still maintaining the perception that all this is outside of us. not our fault. We are rectifying it or balancing it.

In the research I'm working with a friend to prove many women and men who have difficulty with weight are physically carrying their past lives. Many women were pack raped by soldiers, sold as sex slaves for soldiers and sleazy men. These women emotionally built fortresses of fat around their sexual organs, stomach, rear thighs to protect themselves over centuries. When we have to hypnotise them, we have to address all inbuilt anger, guile, rage and pain attached to many of these women dating back to their child hood; However, when you have accessed their past lives the appalling belief systems within these people bewilder even the worst of imaginations. What's more due to their past beliefs, some have had to endure sexual assault in this life too. What these sexual assaults were revealing was this was an atrocious insult from their history.

Many of their bodies started putting on weight at puberty. In society today both men and women make obese people feel horrendously guilty, and that increases their pain however, this is how this pain generates. The attachment increases their weight to protect them at the same time indicating to the judgemental accuser this is your future path. However, unless the victim refrains from believing them and remains in victim mode, their personal judgment will continue burying them deeper into their weight.

This one is a catch 22. By understanding our past history and recognising your opinion of yourself and where we stored it, we can release the guilt that wasn't yours in the first place; it was the offenders, the abusers. However, you believed the abuse then proceeded to ask for more abuse to take place so that you could hide your true pain. This and many addictions are called transference of allegiance. You are transferring your love of yourself or your personal power over to someone else or an imaginary friend. Their love for you becomes the love you believe you deserve. You will then do whatever it takes to acquire it. You will become their insult of you. Their impression of you defines you, personifies you. That addiction is telling you something is out of control. YOU."

I'm working on this book at the moment and it will be called "body of history. So firstly, to all the beautiful people who have difficulty with all forms of addiction, if this is you, on behalf of all the people present, I seriously need you to know, we love you. You are amazing, and if you let go of your victimisation, your addiction has nothing to cling to. That's why it's a catch 22. Your outside world is abusing you because and I iterate this strongly; you are abusing you. Let go of the allegiances. They will never love you the way you want to be loved. There's the answer.

He paused a while then started again, he said quietly, "to help some of you if you are having that problem; one, remind yourself this is not all your fault. Tell your tummy legs thighs any area that you feel you may be using as a fortress; you can tell it to relax now. The battle is over, you're free and it did a good job and is no longer necessary." Some of the audience gave him applause.

"Thank you; now back on path. Now ladies and men but mostly women, you are love. I'm going to emphasise that; WOMEN, YOU ARE LOVE." He laughed as he continued; "Now a lot of the guys may dispute that but I'm sticking by my guns. We have proof. Everything history has to offer says the male species love to fight to win and he is out of control. The proof is in all the destruction and devastation and they are not acts of love. A boys emotional feeling of self, do not develop till much later than a female. I will also say that if you hurt a woman, she has the capability to come at you like a wild cat, but note, I said when you hurt her. She will defend herself and her cubs and loved ones to death, that's love.

What happens when you don't hurt her? Oh yes there are narcissistic women but I'm talking generally; you treat a woman well you get unbelievable LOVE in abundance. Now what I want to do is show women how to take that love, expand it, find your inner soul and join with this love as if it was your dream partner and watch what you can create from it. Watch what comes to you without asking.

We were never meant to be separated or divided. We cannot work when you are separated. Individually when men and women are working in a competitive situation, it never works out. Why, because the rules don't change. Bottom line is; the most physically stronger will win. That's sad. The principle that the only way we will win as a world is, if we bully our competitor into submission. From the naked cave caveman to the dressed caveman.

As ethereal beings our gender may alter but the basic destructive rules remain the same so it doesn't matter who you put in charge it will always be the same. When put in defensive mode we physically fight.

But and this is a big butt; when you are joined, you attain everything and more; why, because you are creating with a mind of united love; the magic wand of the universe. This pleasure of being with another, defines the outcome. The emotion which wasn't there before you joined forces is now the force that creates the future path, only now it is intensified because two of you are doing the same thing with the same force.

For the next forty minutes he spoke of all the possibilities of what happens when you use this universal power of the soul; how like attracts like and how you don't have to look for it; it finds you. By creating in your mind, the final outcome and remaining focused on that outcome, it comes to you with all the accessories needed to be successful at it.

"Now I'm not telling women to leave their husbands; that's the furtherest thing from my mind. If you are not with your soul mate this time but you make a go of your relationship, what you are both doing is creating the future path of happiness with your soul mate in your future life. If your partner doesn't comply don't feel guilty you now know the issue is with you not him or her. How you handle that is your decision but after our break we'll go into it in more detail. Wow doesn't time fly. Okay you have an hour and be back here at ten to.

CHAPTER 7

SECOND BREAK

Jai covered a lot of material in that set but he has so much more to say and he has to make it count. The last session has to be climatic. He cleared his head and prepared himself for the onslaught.

As he walks out on the stage, the band is playing "Nothing's gonna stop us" and the audience are on their feet, swaying and clapping as they sing the words that are displayed on the back screen.

"Okay are we all back. Some stragglers are still trying to find their seats. No that's okay I'll wait." He addresses some of the audience and asks, "How is the food?" They are nodding and all in agreement that the catering was excellent. "Great; enjoying yourself?" Many smiled and nodded, while a couple of females passed some exhilarating and suggestive comments. He raised his eyebrows and smiled, then winked and said "Nah I'm spoken for; but thanks for the offer nicest one I've had today." He paused a while longer.

"Everyone seated," he raised his voice "let's bring this home. The answer to all our challenges is our lack of self-love within us. Unconditional love is the love of our maker as it was called in the sixties and has remained the colloquialism to date. It's what creates everything. You can't exist without it. Hate, anger, rage, wrath, jealousy, envy and all the ongoing emotions are all created from this original love, that's why the balancing of these emotions is also out of love.

Nothing exists without it; it simply takes on another interpretation of it. However, what I am saying here is; the separated interpretation of this form of love which has been displayed by us in patriarchal form for hundreds of thousands of years has resulted in our outcome today and it isn't good enough. We want more; we want better and now we know how to get it.

The obvious conclusion is this dimension we exist in is very Yang male dominant orientated. It is dead set boys and their toys. War games, gladiators, male dominance, football, lessors are subservient, lack of care for other living creatures land and the environment; it is a very destructive selfish narcissistic 'I' orientated nature.

Knowing that the universe is a balanced system that would mean there is another dimension that is Yin female orientated. The other synopsis that other great hypnotherapists have discovered is when we are having a life between life sessions some indicating we alter dimensions. Now I cannot state that this information is either correct or incorrect but I'm going to leave that with you to think about. This could explain the 'utopia theory.'

Not one of my clients has experienced any of these factors but that doesn't mean it doesn't exist." Jai nods with the women in the front row, "you should join my family at xmas our conversation across the dinner table will blow you into the next lifetime." He laughs as he continues.

"What has been proven is that when men rule it is devastating and destructive. When women rule, it is still under patriarchal law as well. The men then take back the territory and then force us to return to an even older patriarchal anarchy. This is proven so often in politics throughout history. Cleopatra is a wonderful example of this so is Akhenaten and Nefertiti. When a female leader wins and rules, within a short period she is ousted and male dominance takes over again and we return to the even older dominance of ruling.

What does this prove? It proves that individually we are useless; together we are a force to be reckoned with; when we are united as one and not separate entities of male and female but together as one, we are unstoppable. In Sleepless in Seattle she says our hands are joined so you could not tell where his started and mine ended this is the oneness. You combine as one unit of unconditional love. Your mind body and soul are one.

The Prophet

   This puts a hole in the story of Adam and Eve. All through our history this story has been deemed as the beginning of time and the woman is deemed as the purveyor of destruction. But history proves another tale. History proves that it was male who created the separation. He adopted an ego, assumed superiority, he wanted to rule on his own and have all obey his call. You cannot begin to imagine the emotion that cause this destruction. All of them, the entire 444,000 of them." He got a reaction from the front row. " He laughed as he added, "yes that true and that is only one emotion." He verified.

   " From that period on, like all narcissists, 'if they cannot control you, they will control how others perceive you.' Now the controversy is, Constantine introduced the Edict of Milan in 324AD which introduced Moses, who supposedly wrote Genesis. Moses annihilated the female gender and all other beings; then had the audacity to bring a god down to his level, the level of man. When you read some of the disconcerting comments taught about women and subservient humans dating back thousands of years if they weren't so abominatingly disgusting they'd be humorous. Saints call them bile of humours, excrement, vomit, and shit. Saints!

   Want more? I promised you this. Some are unbelievable and these are from men with infamous reputations throughout history.

   The original Martin Luther, the leader of the reformation and the Lutheran church. "The word of God is clear; women are meant to be either wives or prostitutes.' Where in the hell is that written? The word of which god?" he paused to let them absorb such a comment from a person they used to respect.

   Jai continues: This one is from a German scholar. Their narrow mindedness and fear continue. 'When a woman has scholarly pursuits there is usually something wrong with their sexual organs." He paused and smiled as he continued.

   The French and little Napoleon" he shouts. "Women are meant to be our slaves; they are our property."

   How about this one? Forgive me, I can't believe men even think this way. Norman Mailer; "A little bit of rape is good for a man's soul" Jai shakes his head. "I wonder if he would he feel the same way if he were on the receiving end of that assault?" There was an applause from up the back of the audience. He raised his hand in acknowledgement.

"I have a couple of beauties you'll love, ready?

"Confucius. One of the greatest gurus of all times." he pauses. "It is the law of nature, not god or the universe, nature," he stressed, "that woman should be held under the dominance of man… or…. one hundred women are not worth one single testicle.' This man put a lot of value on his privates" He laughs in astonishment.

There are hundreds of them but this is the last one for today.

Pat Robertson; he obviously loathed the liberation movement of the sixties. 'Feminism encourages women to leave their husbands; kill their children; practice witchcraft; destroy capitalism and become lesbians.' So, if you were a feminist god help the rest of us. I swear if his wife supported the movement, she must have wanted to hit him over the head with a frypan," he laughed.

The point is these attitudes gave them the right then and now in the middle east to pack rape women and young girls, and babies, enslaved them, belittled them, abused them, and you wonder why they're fed up. I would be too. There is nothing on this earth or any other planet that states anywhere that this attitude toward any other gender is acceptable and although I am emotionally reacting and I'm sorry, and although I have to allow it, the only reason I'm allowing it is because here today I'm giving you the tools to alter it, and create a far better attitude for all beings to exist together equally.

He received a huge round of applause from his audience in agreement. "thank you, we're on the same page , that's great."

My friend whom I confer with is an avid fan of Albert Einstein, she says her greatest pleasure is that for a short period of time she and he were on the planet at the same time for eleven months; but this is what he says;

"The woman who follows the crowd will usually go no further than the crowd,' meaning they are your victims. However, he also stated, 'the woman who walks alone is likely to find herself in places no one has ever been before." This means those who step out of victim mode and realise you are not your brother's keeper, that you can love yourself and from there others will follow. You cannot love or take care of others it's impossible. Like the little cell in the bubble of water you may have billions around you who think and act like you but you are on you own.

This one I will leave you with, for it epitomises all that we are striving for today. Marilyn Monroe was also another avid fan of Einstein and she says; "Women who strive to be equal to men, lack ambition." That says it all.

So, ladies and gents this is how we get there. Before we travel to our higher level of ecstasy there are rules that need to be acknowledged.

At no time am I telling anyone to leave their spouses, because you have a reason for being with them and because I do not know your entire story, I don't have that right.

And two, to clarify I have my soul mate; I'm already on this journey and I can vouch that even if your soul mate is not with you in this life but you are determining this path to take; your binary or DNA alters to make it happen. You are paving your new path for your future path and all the wonderful things that you want in your future life start appearing now. Don't ask for more. Everything you need will be supplied.

To visually explain; over the last hundreds of thousands of years we have been trying to find our soul mate through a maze or labyrinth. What I'm showing you today is by knowing you have already connected to your true soul mate with your mind body and soul within you, you create a path from inside you straight through the centre of the maze to the light. Then all you have to do is walk it.

As I said, if you feel you are not with your soul mate that emotional disturbance is within you. Your partner is informing you of your blockage. Now that is good too because if you treat them with the love you wish to receive you will receive that love in return. St Frances again; it is in the giving that you receive. You take with you the memories you want to keep. You didn't alter them you altered you.

You start feeling healthier because you are leaving behind your victimised body history. Rule number three and this is important for both men and women. Listen to this, do not misinterpret.

IT ALL COMES TO YOU; DON'T GO LOOKING FOR IT. KNOW YOU HAVE ALREADY RECEIVED IT, AND LET IT ALL COME TO YOU.

You were drawn here today because I am part of your future path. So, if you need to use my teachings, my tapes, and my images to assist you to get to your path, I'm more than happy to assist.

Weird I know but the image of Jesus is used every day for people who believe he will save their souls, and that false Italian image of a man painted 4oo years ago of his supposed existence will be available to them right up to the stage when they find out they don't need an imaginary friend any more. This is when you realise your true God is in every cell of your body, was always with you through all times and you are safe; but you simply had to remember that.

What you are doing is releasing all your past confinements and restrictions. The more you release the more others will resurface. How? Through friends, family, work mates and work enemies. Enemies are your most treasured asset. They tell you the worst part of yourself that you have to release. If they or others keep returning you haven't fixed it. They are not your enemies they are your feedback, so avoid reacting to them and fix you. Don't kill your messengers.

The partner you are with now is with you for a purpose. If your partner is having incredible difficulty with weight or anger and you no longer find he or she sexually attractive there is a definite reason within you, not them. You don't find them sexually attractive, there's you answer within yourself. Let me help you fix that. You are following in their shoes and someone is following in yours. So, I put it to you instead of judging and criticizing what would you want the person who is following you to do for you. Then you do it. This is respect, this is equality." The audience was quiet and still, absorbing every word.

"You are here because you want to abridge that emotional status of your relationship with you. Remember what I said. Your past life defines your appearance now. Your appearance now is explaining your relationship with you, not others.

If the body surrounding you looks like The Michelin Man, or you possess a huge sugar belly or tummy; you are protecting a component of your soul and body that has been severely hurt. The reason you are with your partner is more than likely to balance that pain.

You may not be able to move ahead until you have bridged this obstacle. The bigger the body the more series of encounters to this pain you experienced over centuries.

Due to the practices of the time, men may have had to hide their guilt for they had feelings for women and were informed that this behaviour was abominable and they would go to hell; so, they created hard core attitudes so they wouldn't feel the love they wanted most. They were told it was dirty, evil or they would burn.

History has shown that over centuries man has advanced to the hatred which induced the brutal violent behaviour to women by burning them to the stake, drowning them or raping them, and babies to save their souls. So, in front of you is the proof of your past life beliefs. You may need a lot of sweetness to cover your personal hatred or loss of control and personal power.

What that means is that your partner may not be your soul mate but you both may have past issues and by both of you raising your vibration to release all past anguish, pain and victimisation and this unification for both of you will release all of it to give you both the most amazing future life with someone who adores you. You no longer have to be enslaved in this hard-arduous toil of the material world, because you are creating a far better future for both of you in your next life." He paused and took a drink.

"The same way you are using me as the tool to assist you to get to your higher level; maybe I should have rephrased that, but you know what I mean."

He laughed as he tried to continue. "Very difficult to talk sex without getting into trouble; but my point is by recognising that you may be responsible for another's pain and they are in front of you informing you of that maltreatment you created, when you both relinquish the pain within both of you; you will find unconditional love for yourselves and your partners, all of them.

That journey will attract to you your true soul mate in your next life because you have and will be altering your DNA from your past life binary to a brand new one, and the bonus is while you are here you create loving relationships with the people you are with, cleaning your slate of any other obstacles.

Due to prelife plans, your true soul partners will most likely be doing the same thing. If you do not pave the path to them without obstacles, you will have to return to balance the obstacle so you can be together. This new path may incorporate you dying early with your partner as a parent. There is no purer love than the love of a parent for a child and this is the strongest healing grace we can acquire.

This plan is not to have women supersede men, it is to have women leave the subservient dimension of abuse and place themselves above their abusive dimension. From there they are to raise the men to join them so you can all create together. Women are already love and as the very essence of the love they create to unite with their soul mates, family, children, grandchildren, neighbours and the postman, sensually, sexually and biologically. You are to imagine that you are in love forever and from there create it. Create what? Create love forever. Wow! my Byron is coming out." He laughs at his poetic euphemism.

"How would that feel? Absolutely freakin' awesome. Every day of your life is magnificent, and without a lie even if you are single, the most amazing things start coming to you; money, material things, health, beauty, an amazing sense of freedom, all the things you will need for your journey. And you start losing weight. " He snaps his finger "just like that. Then you like the new you, the you want to be so you now have the courage to not only lose more weight but it stays off. You are no longer victim to your false beliefs. Your new beliefs are telling you that you look amazing and beautiful. Welcome to the world of self-love, it is very empowering, and you can't wipe the smile off your face.

Don't ask for it. If you find you are asking for more, you are caught up in the second layer of the man-made material world of lack. So, you are actually becoming a victim to your perception of more lack. Raise you stakes, raise your energy and be grateful for everything.

The beauty of that is you really do not know what you need to progress. You may think its money, but what you truly need is a creative outlet. You may need less. I treated a patient who wanted to give up smoking. When he did, he lost his job, his house, and had to leave town. He took a lessor paying job, bought a nicer house and has far more time with his loving family. He is extremely happy, but he had to lose his material attitude to achieve it.

If you try to control your material world you are no better than the person with the weight problem. Instead of accumulating body weight you are acquiring material fat. You are still hiding you soul within an artificial source. You may actually be missing out on the most amazing experience This path is the way back to acquiring the ultimate happiness not only for this life but your future lives as well."

Jai continued talking for over an hour then he was informed it was windup time;

"Wow time flies I hope I have covered all your questions; so, from me and my team we want to wish you nothing but excellence in your life and future lives. My book has more in depth means of what your can do to achieve higher levels of joy and happiness in your life. It is on sale today out in the foyer with 30% off; it is signed along with tapes and meditation tapes to assist with all your needs to self-love and self-empowerment. I hope you enjoyed our little seminar. I hope it helps you achieve your ultimate happiness for it is achievable for all.

This is not a woman's liberation movement; this is an all equal movement for everybody. History has proven as individuals we cannot achieve our true potential but as one amazing being of both genders the prospects are unlimited.

The band starts returning to the stage indicting it is time to finish. Thank you for being with me today. You have been an amazing audience. My name is Jai Tagore I am a qualified hypnotherapist and past life researcher; it has been an amazing experience; thank you have a safe journey home and goodnight. As he left the band finished with "I wanna know what love is."

As he left the stage, some of the audience came to greet him and ask for his autograph; he was happy to oblige, then he retired to his green room.

There was a sense of relief that it was over but at the same time it was sad. He enjoyed it. It was the longest he had done; He covered a lot of territory and gave hope and hopefully enough curiosity to attract more people next time.

What he had noticed was everything he said he was able to be verified. He was living the life of his dreams. He didn't have to look for it; the paths always opened up to him. The people, the places, everything appeared in front of him.

He too was looking for his soul mate and he knew she existed, but he knew he would find her either in this life or the next. This path he was now walking would bring her to him and he knew he would experience the ultimate happiness and he could feel it now in every part of his body.

Even in his state of bliss menial tasks still had to be done. Time to pack up and take everything back to the studio; he would unpack it tomorrow. He slipped out to see if Jason was still there, he could have done with a nice hot chai but Jason was long gone. He also wanted to congratulate him on an excellent job. He might drive past the café even though it was late.

He packed up his van and drove past the café and saw the lights on so thought he would drop in if he was allowed. Jason opened the door to him; he was happy to see him.

Jason was thrilled with the day's events and was excited to share it with him. All together Roxy, Jason and several staff who helped out had a coffee and laughed and share experiences through the night.

Jai realised this was a promiscuous move on his part but occasionally he would catch glances from Roxy and there was a strong sexual tension between them and he was enjoying it. He noticed her eyes were a strong green hazel. She slouched in a comfortable cane chair still in her apron and work attire looking a little worse for wear and when she laughed, her eyes would sparkle and her hands would dance as she spoke and they entranced him. He noticed he was watching the little things in her now and admiring her more.

About four in the morning he decided to make his exit but was still exhilarated from the previous day's events. He went for his early morning swim and run then off to the studio to unpack his van and file everything away.

Alex arrived also still on a high and still dressed in yesterday's attire. "Don't you have another suit?" Jai sarcastically asked. "You should be proud" retorted a very excited Alex. "You were a hit. This was your best yet. The response was fabulous. They want more books and the women want a lot more of you.

You could have your pick of any of them."

"That's more your areas of expertise not mine. I'm sure you have it covered," was his sassy response. Alex gave a thumbs up.

"We not only cleared all debts, but mate, are you ready for it? Including the band catering and books; we made at least a 60% profit. 60% that's huge, I had to check it twice. Here's all your banking and statements. I've taken out my share. Awesome mate; tell me when you are ready for the next one." He started walking out "oh and we're keeping the caterers. See ya, going home to bed." As he walked out the door he bumped into Jesse. "See ya"

"Yeah bye" responded Jesse. He turned to Jai

"Had a good night hey?"

"Yeah apparently," reacted Jai.

Jesse went into his sound room to apply his incredible talents to the recorded videos from the show. He hadn't done one so long before so he decided to do four discs and streaming instead of the usual one or two. This was going to take a lot of concentration.

Jai didn't have any appointments so he decided to go home and take the day off. He wanted to go the café first, but he knew it was Monday and Roxy had Mondays off so he wouldn't see her so he went home. The weekend's exercise was now taking its toll and he could feel his body starting to drag.

Arriving home in the warm sun he went inside and collapsed on the bed. The warmth satiated the room and stayed for several hours. He was so exhausted dreams failed to appear as he sunk into oblivion.

Over the next few weeks, it was business as usual and the only refreshing nuance in his life was his visits to the café. Now he and Roxy were able to communicate on the regular basis. Einstein stated of the most sensual experience was enjoying an intelligent conversation, Jai was agreeing with this colloquium; he was able to open up to someone who understood and was able to enhance; he was able to exchange ideas, and elaborate more expressively on new ideas. All these sensual conversations were motivating him with exhilaration to write his next book.

CHAPTER 8

ROXY'S REVELATIONS

Jai had a new enthusiasm about his life. He felt vibrant and alive. On Tuesday morning Jesse rushed into the studio, "you have to go to the hospital." He paused to catch his breath. "It's Roxy"

Jai was surprised as he grabbed his coat and keys. "How do you know Roxy? Which hospital?" He ran to his car and quickly jaunted to the hospital.

He raced inside and saw an old friend at the service desk. "Roxy MacLellan?" he asked urgently.

As his friend scanned the patient list "she's in ICU" Jai took off toward the ward, "you can't go in there; it's for family only."

Jai waited outside the ICU when his friend Jesse turned up to sit beside him. "You've got some explaining to do" said Jai accusingly. Jesse handed him a folder. "You need to read this."

"This is a track record," verified Jai

"Yes, it's Roxy's" answered Jesse

"You've been doing past life regression on Roxy without my knowing. Is there some more I should know I thought you didn't want anything to do with her," queried Jai?

"You need to read it" stated Jesse staunchly, "It concerns you. Roxy gave her permission on Monday."

"Monday? Of course, she has Mondays off. So, she spent them with you. Jeez Jesse what else are you hiding?" Jai was releasing his anger at the entire situation.

"They are not going to let you see her, so at least while you are waiting, read," sternly addressed Jesse as he pointed to the file.

Jai wasn't interested, and was ready to place it on the seat beside him when Jesse continued, "I know you love her mate" Jai looked at Jesse defensively "Now see why she loves you" Jesse got up and hastily left.

Those last words rang through Jai and vibrated every cell in his body. "She loves me," he sat in bewilderment. Once he contained himself, he opened the file. He saw that there were 5 past life regressions. The first regression was when she last saw her loving husband and she and the child were lost to the plague. When she died Jai, who was her husband rejected everything that reminded him of her. His pain was so intense and she could feel his pain from the other side but she could not console him; her death was because of the actions he did in the previous life; now in that life he died in darkness.

The regression before that was when she was a victim of the burnings. She had chosen this act of terror to compensate for her previous lives. What was co-incidental was Jai was her persecutor. He was one of the soldiers who arrested her. Alex was the one who sent her to the fires along with others. She was in her early twenties.

Her next regression was of complete anger rage and violence. She was an Asian male soldier, and she enjoyed her attacks for her king and country. She murdered, looted, and swayed her sword with prowess and annihilated any enemy that stood in front of her. She was violently killed in battle around thirty years of age. The sword was thrust through her heart.

In her next regression her rage was wretched. Her hatred personified her body and soul on a path of intense revenge. She again was a male and she slayed all men, all enemies. She was on a path of wrathful anger and pain from her previous life. Roxy could feel this. These two lives were seriously connected.

In the last life she regressed with Jesse, she and Jai were very much in love. His name was Fionn and he was the son of a Celtic elder. They were betrothed and married. During the marriage ceremony they performed the soul ceremony. This is the hands ceremony where they hold hands soul vortex to soul vortex swearing to be soul mates forever. This was the vision Jai saw. As part of the ceremony they both wear heavily donned pure gold rings on their thumbs.

Once the ceremony is over and they are married, they retreat to their abode where they must perform the breathing of his bride. This is where he with his lips touches every part of her body without kissing her. This sensual experience awakens their inner soul. Once that occurs, he is allowed to consummate their marriage. This is the ceremony Jai saw in his vision, he was breathing her.

Before Fionn was betrothed he was taken to the house of his future bride. He had been promised to her older sister. When he was at the house he went up to Roxy and kissed her instead of the older sister. This action created uproar. It was an accident. He didn't know he was supposed to kiss the other sister. Roxy's father started carrying on like a banshee; her mother stepped in and sternly said "I never interfere with the decision of the soul. It is done; Fionn marries Rosa."

This action created envy and jealousy with the older sister who then married Fionn's best friend. After several years of marital bliss there was civil war between farmers. Fionn's best friend betrayed him, and when Fionn went to battle he lost his life. Because there was no son and heir his best friend stepped in and stole the farm, evicting Roxy into the cold. The paid warriors raped and assaulted her before they killed her. This anger then started her rampage of violence, revenge, separation and murder against her sister and all men for several lifetimes.

Jai started moving his fingers the way Roxy does when she talks. He could feel a strange sensation passing through them like a magnetic heat in his fingers. He realised now that when she speaks, she is speaking from her soul. He smiles, it's like the Italians when they speak of food; they use their fingers to express their soulful feelings of the sense of love they feel for their food. Roxy's dancing fingers was her soul connection speaking. He smiled at the beauty of it.

Extraordinary he thought, how she could still remember after 1900 years. His regressions were similar; rage anger war separation, but he'd never seen the marriage. He also knew he lost his wife and child in the plague but the other lives he had no idea they were calibrated with his soul mate.

It was well into the night so he decided to leave. He spoke to the head nurse. She informed him Roxy's daughter had been called and she would arrive the next day. Roxy had a daughter; "what it is with these people no one tells me anything?"

He informed the nurse that he would return tomorrow and she informed him that if she doesn't improve, he will not be allowed to see her, because he wasn't family. He still didn't know what happened.

He was about to lose the love of all his lives and he had no idea why.

He walked to his car and travelled to his house still very unsettled. He found it difficult to sleep. It was a long night of tossing and turning. His bed felt like rocks; it was hard and lumpy and very uncomfortable as if it was trying to evict him. Morning couldn't come soon enough.

Jai had to make an appearance at work but his mind was elsewhere. Jesse simply told him he would not be allowed in to see her, so until he can, just get on with the essential things. If there was any change surely, they would call him. He decided he will call them, but Jesse intervened. "You can't control this; your stress is making it worse for you. Relax everything is as it should be. There's a purpose for this; let it come to you."

Jai knew he was right however; it had been a long time since he felt out of control. Jesse was right he had to let go of his fear. This destiny path has already been determined; worrying fretting is not going to alter anything, but it will determine a frustrating future for him and that is not a path he wishes to travel.

He decided to go to the meditation room and do a really deep meditation to release his anguish. It took an hour and when it was finished his energy level was higher and freer. He allowed what was going to happen, to occur.

It was three days before Jai received a call from the hospital saying Roxy was asking for him. His entire body skipped a beat and he swiftly tidied up to leave to go to the hospital.

"She's in recovery. She's still tired so you can stay a short time," informed the head nurse. He stood outside the window to her room. She was still heavily wired up but talking to her daughter he presumed.

The daughter beckoned for him to enter and he walked around to the door and sceptically entered. Her poor body display a huge trauma of which he still knew nothing. He strained a smile as her daughter introduced herself, "Hi I'm Val short for Valene" He responded "Hi I'm Jai"

"Oh, I know who you are. I'm one of your avid fans, I love your work; been to some of your seminars, love them."

"Thank you I'm honoured. I wish I could say the same about you but I don't know much about Roxy's private life. We mostly collaborate on my work," he hesitantly answered as he tried to civilly converse.

While speaking he realised, he knew nothing about her He knew more about her past life than the one she is actually living.

He knew now he loved her but he knew nothing about her. This created an interesting dilemma. Their conversations were all about how to create better futures; how everything was perfect and the gift of allowing. Before he could go any further with the love of his life there were some areas that needed to be clarified.

Over the next few days, he discovered Roxy has a congenital heart disease and it was hereditary. He sat beside her bed and when alone he held her hand and he would kiss it tenderly over and over again.

In a half sleep stupor, Roxy sleepily told of the story of King Louis of France. "He loved into the hearts and bodies of many women in Paris. He would kiss the back of their hand, then he would kiss their wrist then he would tongue kiss the palm of the hands of the ones he wanted in his boudoir that night. Married or single didn't matter. They say he made love to half the women of France."

Jai continued kissing her hand as she continued. "King Henry the Eighth did the same only with syphilis." Jai started convulsively laughing to himself. Was she aware she told him that story or not? She appeared to be asleep.

He held her hand to his face and watched her rest as he kept remembering her humorous tale. He would use that one day somehow, he would put that into one of his seminars. He would come in for an hour or so every day and sit with her. As she started to recover, he knew he had to do something.

Her daughter is overly worried this time. She wanted to take her mother back to her home town and put her in to a nursing home. She doesn't want to take care of her. She has too many commitments but this way she won't have to worry about her being so far away. Within days she had gone back to her home town to make arrangements, against Roxy's wishes. Roxy does not want to leave her bay, she's happy here responded one of the nurses.

Over this period Jai made some serious decisions. He doesn't think Roxy will agree either but he truly wants to give it a try. He told her about a proposal he had and told her to think about it. Days later he walked into the hospital and Roxy was being checked out and her daughter was beside her, ready to take her home to pack so she can leave. There are no rooms vacant yet so her mother will have to stay with her daughter until one becomes available.

Jai walks up to Roxy and stood directly in front of her. He assists her out of the wheel chair. He runs his fingers down her arm to her fingers as he bares his soul in her eyes. He smiles as he musically plays with her fingers. She recognises the signs, "Do you want to go with Val or come with me?" he whispers. His deep ebony eyes met hers and she felt him reach deep into her soul. She said nothing. Her daughter started objecting. "I'll take care of her" he seductively whispered as he placed his arms around her and led her out of the hospital.

Nothing was said as he took her to his home and placed her things in the spare room. She stood in the centre of the house, and he returned to her. He placed her face in the cup of his hands gently brushed his lips across hers. Tears well in her eyes; he kissed her eyes, her cheeks, then pulled her closer to him as he places his lips on her moist soft mouth. They fell into an embrace, and then she whispered. "You're going have to do better than that."

He stepped back and looked. "I have wanted you to do that for months. Now I find out it has been almost 1900 years I've been waiting."

She slides her hand up the back of his neck, "I see you've been doing some reading." She slides her hands into the base of his hair and tauntingly whispers "I want you to kiss me into next week."

This time he couldn't stop himself. Every part of his body joined hers as his mouth explored hers over and over again.

"You've got a bad heart" he whispered as he tasted her neck

"Your point" and they osculated again with every part of their bodies as he guided her to his room.

He wanted to saver every part of her and she wanted to satiate him. She felt him touch her, kiss her, devour her, over and over again.

For the first time in his life he was completely happy. He lay with her, holding her, embracing her and he still wanted to crush her passionately. Her eyes, her face, her kisses, simply left him craving more.

"Stay with me" he implored.

"Yes" was her over eager response. "Oh yes."

After a while he ran his hand over her forehead "How ill are you?"

"You mean how much time do I have? No one really knows. A while if I'm good," she paused "but I'm not good. I collapsed because I was tired and I had a turn. They happen, it's my life, and I'm used to it."

"But you had a heart turn" stressed Jai in concern.

"Yes and no, I'm okay. I'm not going to stop living because my body suffers from ticks. I'm fine really; I'm going to die yes but I'm going to live first. Don't be scared, don't, don't see me as dying, I couldn't stand that; I'm not dead man walking, that's how Val looks at me."

He kissed her completely on the lips. He could do that. Having her here now he could cherish that always.

In the outside room Roxy's phone was ringing in her handbag. "That'll be Val; she won't be impressed. You don't say no to Val."

"I'll get it for you." He rolled off of the bed and walked toward the other room as Roxy views the magnificent beauty before her, "WOW" she thought; "holy f… he's gorgeous." Jai returned with her mobile and grabbed his robe and he went outside to let her talk to her daughter.

He went into the other bedroom and open up the drapes and windows to let air and light into the room. This all seemed so right; he hoped the daughter wouldn't make trouble. He didn't expect any of this. He was simply going to ask her to stay with him maybe until a better plan could be made. Everything fell in place and came to him. This was not only his life now but his future life and "YES" this is what he wanted. This was more than what he wanted.

He returned to his room and asked Roxy "do you have a robe?"

"In my case"

He returned with her robe then let her freshen up. She entered the kitchen where Jai was floundering around creating a meal. She jumped up into Jai's arms and begins kissing him again. He pressed her up against the larder and penetrated her into orgasmic exhilaration. His body was doing things he had never experienced before. He'd been married; he'd had girlfriends; but nothing like this.

How do you return to normal life after this? They stayed near the larder and started kissing and calming down. They needed to make arrangements but first, the daughter, "what about Val?"

"I told her I was staying in the Bay with you, she could do whatever she liked but I was staying put. We said goodbye and she hung up."

"This is what you do when you get your own way? He suggestively responded. She smiled broadly as she bit her bottom lip and snuggled into him.

"Oh, I am so going to spoil you," he whispered as he tantalisingly seduced her mouth and completely embroiled her in his kiss, sliding his hands over her back massaging every inch of her body.

He placed her on a stool then he went back over to the stove top to start preparing more of the meal. Roxy walked over and snuggled into his back. This was her future life; it was more than she'd ever imagined. She felt like a silly school girl running away from home. She felt free and happy.

She realised now that she always thought she was living under the suppressive censorship of her ex-husband but she was living under the same suppressive objection by her children. Now she was doing what she wanted. They were using their fear of her illness as a means to control her life. Now she finally felt free of all their victimisation.

She could return to light duties at the café, and stay with Jai. Maybe she'd sell her little unit, but she'll worry about that later. For now, she was the happiest she has ever been, holding this beautiful man whom she had loved for centuries, and it all felt so right.

CHAPTER 9

LIVING THEIR PATH

Adjustments had to be made due to this impulsive situation but Jai didn't want the new situation to become difficult. This was the premonition of his future lives. What he wanted in his future life was being prepared now; he had to get it right. He wanted to be with this awesome woman for all time. She made him smile all the time. He felt more liberated than he has ever felt before. He adored her and everything about her, it was the weirdest sensation; weirder that usual.

Now he was walking and holding her hand and he felt this amazing connection. He felt the soul mate connection; it was real. He wanted to know more and he felt Roxy knew. She was teaching him about all the old connections to the soul sensually and sexually. He knew there had to be a huge connection to the sensual love, but sexually?

Women are the flowers that creates life, however the male like the bees and insects propagate the flowers that needs to be fertilise. Sex is an important part to the ongoing unison evolution of the universe. It was the separation and division of the union that destroyed our planet. This unison creates the ultimate bonding.

Laughter, happiness, joy and bliss exploded from these two and everyone noticed. They took care of all the menial tasks and both tried to remain normal but it was truly impossible; they were living their belief of unconditional soul love and it was extraordinary. In this place of higher energy everything they needed became available without any worry, anxiety or stress. Jai taught this, but now he was the living proof of his teachings.

He woke up alive and excited about his existence. Roxy returned to work and helped Jason run her café without pressure or worry. Was this existence real and if so, why isn't everybody living it?

This was Roxy's question. How did this fallout start? Why would someone choose such misery over the unbelievable joy she and Jai were living? Is it possible that not everyone has a soul partner? That would explain the division and separation.

Like her past life regression when Jai chose her over her sister because their souls stepped up; her sister then married his best friend but they weren't soul mates. Their marriage was one of material legislation. Did these people then decide the rules of the road, because they didn't believe in soul mate destiny, because they never experience it? She spoke of her concerns to Jai and in his research, he had never asked this question so it would be only speculation.

This initiated the other question as to why didn't she come to Jai when she wanted the past life regressions.

"When I first arrive in the Bay, I was on my way to work and I accidently touched someone's hand and I collapsed, and hid around the corner, I thought it was you." she explained Jai concurred that the same thing happened to him. Roxy queried "what did you see?" He explained "the face of a beautiful woman who was his bride; and he had this overwhelming sexual sensation to kiss her and make eternal unrelenting love to her into the next time zone; but we had to finish the ceremony and hold hands. I had a thick gold ring on my thumb."

"The 'opening of the soul' ceremony; the dedication of soul mates to each other," she smiled as she concurred. She walked around to him and took his hand, and then she started playing his hand like a guitar. She caressed the back of his hand, then the front, then the centre of the palm, and then she gently kissed the centre of his palm.

Very hesitantly Roxy explained, "I didn't see that. I saw when you murdered me," she paused. " I didn't know if you were a friend or an enemy. When Jesse came into the café I asked if he worked with you and I needed help. I told him I didn't want you to know. So, he took me to a hypnotherapist by the name of Gary."

"Gary? He took you to Gary? Who did you work with?"

"Jesse did it, we simply used Gary's studio, why?"

"Gary is my son." He paused. "He took his mother's name. How many more people know about this?"

"No more." Then she continued "then in the second of my regression sessions I discovered that you were protecting me from being burned to death, so you lanced me because the fires took hold too fast and they couldn't reach the rope. Apparently, we agreed that you would do this; that path was to start me back to you.

Yet in the last regression where we got married, your friend Alex was the one who married my sister and betrayed you for your property. He was also the one who arrested me to get burned. The rage, anger and hatred for that man started me on a path of wrathful revenge. It took centuries to overcome. I didn't know you were the one I loved; what I saw you were here to slay me again." She paused a while then continued.

When I saw you lose me to the plague you were inconsolable. I was still there in spirit trying to show you I still loved you but you hated everything I showed you. You cast me out of your life. You hated me due to your pain. I didn't want that to happen again. I thought if we never met you wouldn't go through the pain of losing me again and maybe next time we could start again."

"You prevented that when you started talking to me didn't you?" he smiled as he grabbed her and kiss her on the forehead.

Roxy continued; "You told me we had to start now due to the continuum. If I waited till next time, I would have to go through all the pain I went through this time again to inform me of what I had to do." She slipped her arms around his neck "and I wasn't going to start again I couldn't start again." Then they both embraced in an intoxicating kiss. He held her tight, he wasn't going to lose her again either.

Several days later Alex came around to the studio to do some follow up work and to inform Jai that he was leaving town for a while, and if he needed some help to call his office

As he was leaving, he passed Roxy returning from the café. When he passed her, she felt a horrid chill go through her. She'd seen him a several times at the café, but this time there was something strange.

She made an appointment to see Jesse again. If she had her life taken and her home and money taken, she needed to know the life before that. She needed to know the life that set up these circumstances. She told Jai she was doing this and as Jesse was her therapist, she wished to continue with him. He agreed but now she could do it in his studio.

Roxy slipped under very easily and when she transgressed back, she returned to her marriage. Then to the betrayal, from there she digressed back another lifetime. In this lifetime she was a hard-working woman who took care of her father.

Her brother was a lay about who spent his allowance on sex, women, drugs and gambling.

When her father passed away the entire inheritance went to her brother and his whore of a wife. These were the rules of the land to maintain the property in prosperous sted. Her loathing of her brother and his disgusting behaviour was her driving force.

Roxy married well and when her father's property was in a devalued state, she and her new husband bought the estate and threw her brother and his wife out in to the street and returned the estate back to prosperity. Her brother was found murdered and his wife was destitute and died soon after.

When she woke up, she recalled what she saw; this was the reason for all the barbaric actions of her future lives. Her narcissistic material jealousy was to be her demeaning force. She allowed the political belief systems of the time to define her future lives.

This man-made imprisoning factor destroyed her life for more than 2000 years. However, now because she understood she was able to release the rage, anger and wrath to Alex for all his lifetimes of abuse. She had to learn to release the narcissistic component of her inner self. Now she understood Val and why she was in her face. Roxy shared her experience with Jai and asked if Alex had ever married.

"Alex had a wife and child somewhere up state; he never appeared to have found a soul mate. He was always there for me but no women were ever seen by him." Jai responded as he prepared dinner, "Alex doesn't believe in this stuff, he just makes money from it."

"Some things never change" laughed Roxy.

All these new experiences needed to be written down, so Jai made a huge decision. He was going to become a full-time author. He had sufficient funds to live on comfortably. He was considering giving his share of the hypnotherapy studio to his son. He could work with Jesse.

This gave Roxy the same idea. She would leave her café to Jason instead of her daughter. This way it would stay open in the Bay. Jason and Jonah loved it and it would fulfil their dreams. He's already managing it and learning new recipes to test on customers. Her daughter would only sell the place because she doesn't like it and she only wanted the money. So, Roxy made arrangements to allow Jason to expand his business prowess and take over the café full time.

Jai had one more major proposal to carryout. He created a simple beautiful onyx ring for him and her. Roxy loved onyx, it reminded her of his eyes; the deep black depths of the universe looking back at her. He designed the rings in yin and yang of black and white onyx, soul mates forever.

He prepared a romantic dinner, softened the lights played her favourite songs and all was set. Roxy walked in and was completely overwhelmed.

He served up her special dinner, danced with her close to him and as he kissed her on her neck, "Marry me please, just marry me." He paused and waited " love you so much."

She whispered, "I love you too, but a wedding?"

"I know; that's why I only want a small wedding on the pier, you me and a minister. Jesse and Jason can be our witnesses. I don't want the fancy stuff I only want you. If you want a party afterwards I'll organise one for you, but I just want you now and forever, does that make sense?

I don't want to lose you again, let's do this for us, forever," he pleaded as if his heart would break if she said no.

"You've really been thinking about this haven't you?" She smiled as he took her hand

"That's a yes?" he questioned with a smile.

He slipped the ring on her finger and she gasped with joy. It was absolutely beautiful. Now everything was complete as they continued to seal the pact with a slow night of sensual, sexual consummation.

Come Friday the four of them went to the registry office. The ceremony was more paper work then fancy church ceremony, however, they did repeat vows with a celebrant on the pier on Saturday. Jason prepared a small soiree for Roxy and some of her friends from work.

Jai's son Gary and Jesse were in attendance as well. It was a simple night with friends who loved them.

They were able to complete each other more now for Jai didn't have to leave the house. He set up an office full time to write. He had too much happiness to share and the words kept over flowing. He found himself repeating himself. There was no rush but he needed to be active.

He was now living his teachings from the conferences and seminars. He knew he would but thought it would occur in his next life. He only had to imagine it being perfect and by focusing on that the rest would happen, but this was so much more than happy ever after, this was happy ever now.

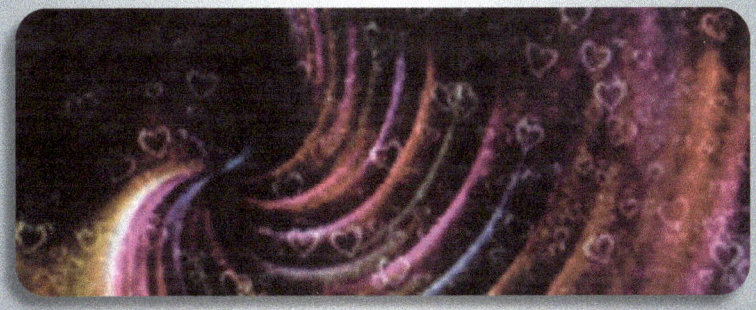

He decided to call his seminar "Happy Ever Now."

What's more he was going to do it with his wife; he was taking her on the road with him. He spoke to Alex but he was unavailable. He recommended a work associate within the company to organise it.

This was to be the proof of all his previous teachings. This was the seminar of seminars. He was going to show the world that his philosophies were correct. When you dream of achieving the most beautiful relationship with your one true soul mate; when you focus on that dream every day of your life with your every breath knowing that it will come to you, watch what happens and stay alert!

CHAPTER 10

TEACHING THE PATH

Jai spent all his time with Roxy, formatting his new program, and their love together exploded to higher levels of consciousness. They shared everything together; their walks, their coffee, their friendships with others. They wrote continuously of the experiences they shared and how he felt every minute of being with her.

Yes, when he began his path of creating what he dreamed would happen, all these special moments were an integrating component. He focused on touching her, kissing her, loving her, being with her every moment. She loved his work and he loved hers. He would be able to communicate with her and she with him. He left nothing to chance. He even incorporated how she might look; how soft she would feel and how she responded to his touch.

This seminar was going to be an introduction of the audience to Roxy. He wanted the world to know she was his soul mate and how he found her and how they can have the same amazing relationship with the ones they love and if they don't have that person yet he will show them how to achieve this amazing unconditional love.

The promoting company had him booked to perform out of town in a large stadium which was unusual but it had a stage so both he and Roxy would be performing together. It had one screen behind him that he could use for his power point.

While Roxy was away Jason would take care of the restaurant it was only overnight on the weekend. It was a sold-out venue but what the promoting company did was a send out a status feedback forms to understand the variability of the audience.

They did this through arranging a weekend stay at a specific motel. They were able to define the type of audience interested in this seminar so they could promote to that specific audience in future.

Sixty percent of the audience were single or divorced both male and female. Others were married with friends and a few couples. To the promoting company this meant these people were looking for their soul mates and others were trying to enhance their relationships with their soul mates now.

Everything else was like a normal seminar. Jai requested an early evening event, nothing extravagant. He knew what he wanted to say and how he was going to say it.

First of all, he would revise how everything is exactly how it should be to substantiate the art of allowing.

Secondly, he wanted to revisit his buddha theories of all around you is actually feedback of your past existences and why we are where we are now. We have to recognise that everyone is here with the best intentions.

Next, he would then explain how we from a new perspective can start loving ourselves, empower ourselves and create existences beyond our wildest dreams. We have to start releasing our victimisation from everything and everyone and rescue us first. Then we will have the ability to really start loving ourselves. He will explain that this is the hardest transition. Once we learn that we are entitled to be loved not only by us but by others and as such, create an entirely new world of that same love, then, we can focus on our attention on our extraordinary life with all the special people, places and things whom we wish to share all our lives with.

As with his previous seminars he will speak of how we have rendered our own ability to love by dividing the very power we have to create from, our source, in half. It's like breaking our magic wand in half and expecting it to maintain full impact to give us all our needs, then wonder why it backfires. Jai does all this and his audience as always become completely engaged in his philosophies. Now it comes to the newer part of the program. The part that he has never shared before. Roxy's debut as his sidekick.

She knows her work as she has done platform before but not to such an enormous crowd. She knew what she had to say. She knew what she had to do. Her goal is to empower both genders to being the most amazing beings they could ever perceive. If she could reach one then she would be a success, for he or she would take it forward to others and that gift would open the doors to those who are following her.

Her dad was a drunk and he died early in her life, leaving her with a very angry mother. His future path would be harsh but Roxy would be his endgame. She can't walk his path for him but she can make his final endgame and future path worth it. She has to be the best she can be and show other's how to achieve the same remarkable happiness. This is her goal, to empower women and show them how to attain true freedom.

Jai has to now introduce his lovely wife and he apologises for her luggage was lost at the airport so Roxy had to acquire new clothing for the presentation. He gratefully informs the audience that some of the staff from the resort volunteered to assist her in buying some attire from some of the fancier stores in the town and he thanks them for their kindness in advance. "should I be worried?" he queries the front row and they shake their heads.

"It was perfectly okay" he jokes "I gave her my credit card." The he pauses for a while, " Oh, I have no problems giving Roxy my credit card. There's nothing on it." he and the audience enjoy his humour, as he laughs at his own joke. "No flies on this joker," as he winks to his audience.

"Ladies and gentlemen, it is my greatest pleasure to introduce to you, my beautiful mentor, friend, teacher and wife of twelve months now. May I present my beautiful Roxy Tagore." As the audience stands and applauds.

Roxy make her entrance and Jai stands on the other side of the stage in awe of what he is seeing. There is a long pause as Jai stares at the wonder of what just walked on the stage.

"WOW!" he pauses again. " This staff has out done themselves."

Roxy walked out in a snug fitting off the shoulder floral dress, her short hair softly flowing and red stiletto shoes.

Jai was taken back at how stunning she looked. He stood there with a grin on his face from ear to ear. He demonstrated to the audience how he was stunned at her outfit.

"Wow!" he shook his head and laughed as the audience laughed at his reaction. He cleared his throat and smirked at her some more, and as he started pointing to the dress he asked; "Are we allowed to keep that?" he laughs at his reaction and enjoyed the moment.

Roxy shyly giggled for she was hoping it would make an impact, but this was more than she expected.

Now she was slightly embarrassed.

He breathed out a heavy sigh "You've never dressed like that for me?"

"It'd be a waste of time" she quietly responded as she covers her mouth to embarrassingly laugh.

The audience bellowed with laughter along with all the staff. Jai cripples over with laughter at her unexpected comment.

Through his laughter he jibes, "I hope they never find your luggage," as he still looks at her in utter amazement.

He laughed as he continued, "darling, you'll never be able to walk in those shoes."

Roxy nodded in agreement and mimed "I know."

He walked over to her, embraced her tightly and gave her a gentle kiss, as he commented "you're the same height as me; You look utterly amazing. I so totally adore you," and he embraced her again and she echoed his words.

"I don't know what you've done with my wife but if you ever want to remarry me, I'm available," he laughs as he kisses her again. "Wow"

With his arm around her waist he walked her to the centre of the stage again and tried to continue. He laughed with her and she placed her head on his shoulder. He clears this throat to begin again.

"When I started teaching the unconditional love emphasis about fifteen years ago, I was building from the 'if you can dream it you can be it concept.' It wasn't until I met Roxy that she informed me of the breaching of our very existence in rendering our initial being in half and separating us from us that I was able to understand why we constantly kept creating more pain for us to endure. Why we couldn't understand that the pain we saw in the world was reflecting the very same pain within us. She taught me that we will do, buy, become addicted to anything outside ourselves to fill the void so we don't feel it anymore. Anything from a bird to a mansion."

Roxy kissed him on the cheek and went back to a chair which was bought on stage for her to sit on during the seminar so he could continue his work. "I have to be truly honest here; this woman is my best mentor, best friend and one hell of a lover. The reason I tell you this is because that is what we walked away from. I don't know why we would do that, other than maybe vanity ego pride, and thought we didn't need our partner, thought we could do it all by ourselves. I don't know the original reason. What I do know is when we stop victimising ourselves, when we return to our true nature of self-love and self-empowerment, the magic, the unbelievable bliss that fills your life, is something you cannot imagine.

That's it, you cannot begin to imagine the almost fairy tale existence that enters your life. I would see it in others who had found their soulmates and they would talk to me for my research and I would almost think they were making it up to impress me, but they weren't, and now I'm living it.

We as in Roxy and I asked this horrid question as to why would we choose the other path and we have only one explanation and it is only a probability not fact, but it is based on tests done in the middle of last century

Roxy is an avid fan of Albert Einstein and in one of her stories she tells of how his heart broke when scientists split the atom. The concept that scientists would dissect anything that would create the total destruction of any other living thing on earth painfully hurt him. He would say how he detested how countries would dress up their men and send them off to another country under the thesis of what was to perpetrate the act of murder on innocent men, women and children, and now to create the most destructive means to wipe out nations under the guise of war was horrendously unacceptable. His opinion of the destruction of Germany, Hiroshima and Nagasaki was heart rendering.

The same destruction that we as human beings are experiencing is of the same benevolence. We split our atom; the divided the union of the human soul construction and it is now destroying everything it touches."

He pauses for a minute. "The emotion created is the weapon of choice, however we as humans play one side in one existence then the other side in the next existence. One existence we play yin, in the next we play yang, in one we play oppressor in the next we play recipient. However, in all existences we are victim to that emotion we created to divide us, then we look outside ourselves to fill the void of the component of ourselves we are missing. To explain this further if I may.

The two atoms that were divided were placed in separate rooms. Whatever occurred to one the other reacted in exactly the same way at the same time. When we react to our emotion, we react in exactly the same way regardless of the fact we are yin or yang. We do not alter. Yin and yang are the same only our perception what we are seeing is different. We are using the same energy in the same way. Too heavy?" He pauses a moment. "Someone is in front of you arguing through rage, you retaliate, your emotions are exactly the same. The side of the argument may be different but the actions demonstrated by both of you are exactly the same. You are one and the same. You are yin and yang as one displaying the same emotion.

Now let me share with you what happens when you both do it together when you are reunited in love. Roxy and I put this seminar together about nine months ago and if I did it solo without her it would have been menial and boring. Her input was vital to its success.

We have identical rings, wedding rings we had them specially designed. Roxy loves onyx, so we designed yin yang wedding rings out of black and white onyx. Jai held up his ring to show the audience and Roxy complied by holding up hers. We decided to reunite us as soul mates for all time. Now here is the irony, we both wore matching Ghetto pants long white shirts and black vest to our wedding ceremony; it was awesome, we looked alike we were one and we were joined as one again physically, mentally and spiritually and stylishly," he jests.

"That's another reason why the shock in the amazing dress. We live at the bay. I've never seen Roxy in dress." He looks back at her and laughs again, "I didn't even know that magnificence creature was in there." Roxy laughed with embarrassment along with the entire stadium again. Jai sighed and caught his breath and started again. "You've been holding out on me girl!" the laughter continued.

"How do you know you are on the right path?" He turned to Roxy smiled and lovingly said "they stand in front of you." He stated adoringly as he smiled at Roxy admiringly and she nodded as she consented to his comment with her agreeing eyes.

"If they are not, check all areas around you. Ask what is preventing it, and learn to listen for the answer. The problem is within you, not others but they will tell you where to look. You may have issues you need to resolved first, fine, but don't lose focus on your final goal. Something is out of control. You're the something's victim.

The guys and girls at work may be jerks then you need to resolve that within you. Is work telling you to move on to a place where you will be more appreciated? If there is a guy or girl and you think you love them but they are part of the jerk syndrome; you may be close but not him or her.

Your answer is to go to a place where you will be treated with the respect you deserve; but that won't happen until you start treating you with self-respect first. Remember learn to love you first. The jerk is treating you that way because you are treating you that way. At no time lose sight of your dream soul mate. Out of the blue someone who looks nicer, acts nicer, and you would think would never talk to you wants to take you out to dinner, this is what we call 'over and aboves'.

You have your aim of Mr or Miss right, you focus on what they will treat you like, how you will feel together, but you never added super god or goddess to the plan, and here they are before you, more than you ever dreamed of." He turns to Roxy and informs the audience, "and she is my goddess."

"By chasing someone like the handsome jerk, all you would have received would have been the jerk and more self-loathing. By allowing the universe to supply your true soul mate and everything that is needed to acquire that, the universe will supply everything needed to keep you on the path. A new town, a new job, new house, money, just allow the flow to take you to your heaven on earth, your Utopia.

Your life up to date has already allowed the river Styx to take you to all the pain you can endure; now allow the universe to supply you with all the joy you think you want and more. You deserve it.

I'm going to hand this over to Roxy now and she will take you on a female's perspective of this journey. Who'd have thought that we think differently?" He turns to his wife and she raises her brow questioning his comment and he responds "viva la difference" kisses her and whispers in her ear.

" OOH lady, you take my breath away. You're amazing," their hands touched and he lets her have the floor.

Roxy gives a sigh and in a quiet demur voice steps up to the microphone and says "Hello, can everyone hear me? The audio department may have to adjust the volume. You may notice I don't own the floor quite as well as Jai and that's fine.

When I would do platform years ago, I used to get called out as prejudice and sexually biased and a woman's liberationist and nothing could be further from the truth. Yes, my objective was to empower women so they would re-empower men and my argument was they will follow if they want to but at the moment, they have life as they want it and many do not want to change.

Let me give you an example. This is not based on fact it was something that crossed my mind many years ago when I was introduced to a barking owl.

Very rare birds but they do bark like dogs and they do it all night. I imagined a neighbour yelling out "shut that flaming dog up" and then the next morning being so tired and angry gets a gun and shoots the neighbour's dog.

The question I'm asking is, how many of you assume the neighbour is a male? Raise hands, come on." Roxy bends over with laughter, "all of you. At no time did I mention the gender or even infer it was male." She tries to continue with a straight face, "why is that do you wonder?

And yes, there are tales that depict females are as well but my point being, we wear specific attitudes which define the character of our gender and they are not sexist or biased." She keeps grinning and states; "That story simply doesn't comply if the assailant is a woman." She paused then introduced her topic. "This is the narcissistic primal instinct. This is the component of "I" and it does exist in all of us. but it has a very strong male bullying violent streak which through history has defined the male oppressor instinct more than female.

In our narcissistic world the attitude of violence is extremely male orientated but here is the irony; if a female is narcissistic, they look for whipping boys to carry out their acts of atrocity. Many horrendous crimes carried out by the gentle men have been brainwashing ly provoked by an extremely dangerous narcissistic minds of a female. These females are born with it. All narcissists are, but psychologist can only allow evidence in this lifetime so it has to be environmental.

Quick story;" she moves beside the dais. "A relative of mine had a naturally born narcissistic child. We all had to attend a party of some description, and one of the guests bought a puppy and placed it in a protective inside kennel away from the family animals as it was a new environment for the puppy.

This child was in the toy room where the puppy was being kept. The child was playing with some toys. He started pelting heavy toys at the puppy. The relative asked the child to stop doing it and to go get his toys and return them to the playing area." Roxy started smiling. "The child gets the toys and stood near the kennel staring at the woman; then he again pelts the toys even harder at the kennel.

I'm watching this in total shock. This child is under two. The woman brings the child out into the dining area where the child then starts hitting the refrigerator and screaming at the top of his lungs. He wants to go back into the toy room. She quietly says no you have to go outside. So, he hits the fridge again. In walks mum; she picks up junior asks what is happening," Roxy raises her voice in aghast "and the child screams as he points to the woman 'she's hitting the fridge,' Roxy laughs. "This child is under two and knows how to outright lie to your face and not flinch.

I'm now totally in shock as the parent takes the child outside as she says 'you shouldn't provoke him.' The child looks back over his mother's shoulder to the woman with the infamous narcissistic smirk as if he had won.

The poor defeated woman sat beside me completely exhausted and commented "well at least he's outside." I couldn't believe what I saw; however, what it did do for me was, prove the environmental theory completely wrong and the ongoing continuum of life theory with more validation. He was good. My goodness, he was very good at what he did, and he knew it.

The environmental theory is reproofed around the continuance of overindulgence of the young spoiled child. This evidence and other evidence I have found is the over indulgence of these types of children is done out of sheer frustration. 'These children do not stop.'

You know the expression 'god always opens another window' well in this case you wish he would shut a few. They find cracks, holes windows, bricked walls weaknesses, vulnerabilities, and they keep going until you relent. You have no choice; they are not taught this; it is natural. One of the narcissistic tales that caught my eye was of an American lad aged seven, whose grandmother would give him the neighbourhood cats and he took pleasure in killing them.

"Wow these shoes." Roxy comments as she starts to stride across the stage. "Great weapon though hey?" she laughs. "When I was young, I would dance in these shoes every week. Bought a new pair every week; couldn't do it now." She laughed with the audience. Then as she indicates her garments; "As you can tell I don't wear these all the time" she laughed. Roxy looks back at Jai who is laughing as he is seated in her chair and she continues.

She indicates to Jai "He's an old man," she pauses and grins, "I have to be careful; I could go up for second degree murder."

She and the audience laugh.

"Imagine me before the judge and he asks 'how did he die' and I answer 'extremely happy.' Roxy clears her throat and turns to see Jai collapsing in his chair with laughter. The audience applauded.

"Sorry a little distracted there; back to it. Narcissist relationships appear to be one sided. All the energy appears to be flowing one way. Recovering from these forms of pain is the hardest to reconcile within one self. The sad part is these relationships are becoming the foremost popular form of relationship breakdowns in society today, be it family marriages, friendships, and be it business and politics. The core of most patriarchal dominance is this narcissistic element. However, both are coming from the narcissist personification. Both parties are using the same vibration to gain their own personal power.

If you have listened to the teachings of Jai you will know that the lemniscate or the infinity sign or karma indicates that this supremist attitude is the downfall of these people for the next life. In knowing this we can prevent the recipient victims from wanting revenge and validation. Let the oppressors build their own graves.

A quote written by Steven Moffat in Britain 'there's no such place a hell, it is 'just heaven' for bad people' the emphasis being on 'just heaven', I thought that brilliant. The more atrocious these people are, the more justice will be born upon them, so don't waste you amazing energy wanting to gain validation which won't be anywhere near as disgusting as what they are creating for themselves to receive.

There is a movie Arthur and the Sword in the stone. In the movie Arthur sees his parents killed by his uncle and he is taken in by prostitutes and raised as their own and he becomes a successful child of the streets. He has to flee and is captured to be one of the prisoners who will try to pull out the sword. He however is successful revealing to the uncle that he is still alive. The uncle asks 'what made you survive.' Arthur then goes through many trials and tribulations but through all of them he hates his uncle; It is not until the end of the movie that the question is answered;" she pauses, then emphasises, 'you.'

This is poignant in our trials today. The tools that hurt us the most are the essential instruments needed to overcome the very things that are holding us back. They are the very tools needed to be successful. These tools are the narcissistic family, friends, co-workers, politicians. All are tools to bring us to the point of awakening, if you like. Awareness is a more resourceful phrase.

By recognising that these tools for want of a better word, some more than others," Roxy laughs, "oh I've had them too and in some cases the word tool is more than apt," she laughs, "we have to actually thank them for every cantankerous action they threw at us, they made us better for it and we are able now to walk away and let them fall where they may with our blessing. We allow them to be who they are and we are no longer victim to them or anyone.

Arthur murders his uncle; well we don't have to be that heroic; we only have to let them go; relinquish our control. Our control helps us maintain our status of victimisation. We keep the injustice. We create new emotions every time we speak for us to experience as victims again. If you want to control anyone, control yourself. A quick example. You go shopping, you have your shopping bags and you load your groceries in your bags an accidently pop something in your handbag as well. When you leave, you go to the next lot of shops and discover you didn't pay for the little item in your handbag. Now you have a choice.

Me, because I know the repercussions of this menial act, I run back to the shop and pay as quickly as possible." She pauses," the ongoing victimisation that this simple act of forgetfulness can cause is not worth the pain it will cause for months on end. People who owe you money, forget to pay. Bills will have an extra twenty percent on them. You will never get a break; you will be victimised in every corner and you will wonder why. Now here are the wonderful avenues of this debarkle. When you return to pay for your article the people who are watching you are following in your footsteps. Because you did this you will have saved them too. That's the way it works, so if you can't do it for yourself do it for those you love who are following you." There was an applause around the audience. "Thank you. That is really appreciated.

Control is one of our worst enemies and if you have experienced narcissism it is a controlling relationship. You fight to gain your control back. It is that control that will ensure you to return to another and another.

If you are tired of the merry go round you have to do it another way. There is another way and as Jai has informed, we are the walking proof.

After I walked out on all and I mean all, family, friends and exes I was standing on my own and the future was what they call in Mahjong the white dragon; an undetermined future. That was me, and as Roosevelt said in night at the museum, 'how exciting!'

Einstein is my hero and his quote saved my life. He stated "The woman who follows the crowd will usually go no further than the crowd. The woman who walks alone is likely to find herself in places no one has ever been before."

I was in that position. I was about to create an entirely new life for me; so, I did. I had been informed of the life I didn't want, so I now had to create one I would want. I had been surrounded people who were so materialistically orientated that they didn't have room to love me, not the way I wanted. If I took all their possessions and money away from them, they would have become the meanest most jealous and envious gold-digging grappling beasts until they got it all back.

Then they would be nice me again, but they still wouldn't love me or anyone for that matter. That was when I realised that without love, the love I wanted the real love, it wasn't worth anything. What I also discovered was, you have everything you need to have all that you need, but you have to listen. But listen to what? No one was talking to me. This answers to the question do you have to give up everything to follow your heart. No, you simply do not have to make the material things the main focus of your life. All will be provided.

I started believing I deserved so much better, and it all unfolded before my eyes. I bought a place to work and met beautiful people who showed me my new direction. My environment altered, my life altered and my love for me altered. I was the happiest I had ever been in my life.

Here's where the fun part starts. I always believed I'd been separated from my soul mate, because I had never experienced love, so I was determined I wanted to find him; not for one-minute believing he exited in my now.

I always perceived he would be in my next life so I imagined being with him in my next life. I imagined formatting all my life experiences in this life and taking them as memories for my next one to return with him there. In imagination we were so happy, always smiling, laughing, holding each other, loving each other with every breath. Oh, I've got a good imagination, but what was taking place was the people around me were experiencing just that form of love in front of me. This is what they meant when they say listen. It's not listen; it's watch. They were telling me what was in store for me now, but I missed it. I still presumed it was for my next life.

I had no real idea what he looked like, I only knew how I felt around him, how I wanted to be treated by him, how I wanted to love him, that's all I knew. I wanted that love, the love I wanted to feel for the rest of my lives.

Once I settled at the bay a lot more was revealed but up until then I was working with imagination only. The magnetic force behind the dreams opened such a huge array of doors and I simply walked into all of them. At no time did I worry about money for all my dreams had been paid for it was simply a matter of allowing it to come to me.

Focus is the main priority; remembering every moment of the path you want to take and watch it fall into place. As Buddha says you are in the world but not of the world. I sound Like Jai." She looks at him and smiles; he responds.

"In other words, the atrocities of the world do not affect you. That is their creations not yours, they are allowed to live their lives that way, you cannot control theirs, only yours. You fly over the maze to your heart's desire. To dream of material things will only bring you things and more emptiness to fill the voids. Voids are results of victimisation. But to dream of the ultimate that love has to offer is to allow the universe to reveal itself to you in unlimited spectacular technicolour. When it all starts unfolding you will get abundant of over and aboves as well."

Over and aboves? came a question from the audience.

"Over and aboves? Umm, bucket list plus dreams come true." A quick little story.

A little boy is with his mother shopping and she is on a tight timetable and has a lot to do. So, she makes a deal with her little boy. You behave and help me get the shopping done I will give you $10 to spend on anything you like. So, not only is he good, he helps her get all the foodstuff she needs and they finish in super early time. The child is lactose intolerant but he is adamant he wants an ice-cream. Mum make another deal. Instead of reacting, she says, well when you are sick tonight, I will stay with you because you stayed with me when I needed you. She goes to the new ice cream parlour and they sell whey ice cream. The boy tries it and likes it. Mum is informed there is no lactose in it. Mum buys him the biggest ice cream sundae with lollies and fruit and chocolate topping especially made for him. She also buys a small one for her. They have a most enjoyable time. That night there was no reaction by the child, in fact he slept soundly and now on special occasions mum and her little boy have a special place to dine. All he wanted was an ice cream. All mum wanted was to get the groceries done quickly. By staying in that place of magical surprises where everything come to you; you imagine your bucket list and you get over and aboves of dreams you didn't even think of. Your WOW moments and there are billions.

The rest is history. As Jai says we received our over and aboves. That's your bucket list with stuff you can't even begin to imagine. Roxy reached for Jai indicating she was finished, "I utterly adore this man and I truly wish you all the same."

Jai walked up put his arm around Roxy's waist and kissed her gently on the lips as he starts his finale.

What did I say; you deserve to be ultimately happy; that's fairy tale stuff.

No fairy tale stuff is happy ever after; after what? We don't do after; we do now. **HAPPY EVER NOW**

We do happy ever now, and so should you. Now I'm going to take this lovely lady home and love her the way she deserves and I want you to do the same with the one you love.

A quick story before we go. When I went to school there was a nasty nerd there who would always made me feel like rubbish, and I hated him because he was a proper ass. In our adult life I use to still avoid or treat this guy as rubbish because in my eyes he was still an ass. Roxy asked me why was I an ass around him? My response was he's the ass I'm not. Roxy pointed out that when I was around him, I acted like an ass as well. Long story short; by changing my attitude to him, he was no longer an ass, and he dropped out of sight.

My point being, if you don't believe the person with you is the right one, maybe it is your attitude to them that is making it so. If they are not right this action will not make any difference. However if they are and you alter you attitude and start treating them as you would like to be able to love your soul mate, and it's your husband or lover or both, he'll probably ask 'who are you and what have you done with my wife?' he laughs, 'but they will respond accordingly. They will become the love of your life. You must love you first, and the rest comes to you.

Ladies and gentlemen, I'm proof that this works. I wish for you all the biggest over and aboves you could never dream of." As he kissed Roxy passionately on the lips in front of everyone, "I wish you this and more. You deserve it and it is out there, now go and dream yours into reality. From Roxy and me good night, we love you, and thank you; to all the staff and promoters who assisted, have a safe night and safe journey home" Both he and Roxy waved as they left the stage arm in arm.

They quietly retired to the change rooms and found that Roxy's luggage had been retrieved "shall I throw it out" mocked Jai as he held her in his arms desiring to kiss her passionately, but knowing the area was too open.

"No" she laughed "I need my shoes,"

As they picked up their gear, they walked to the awaiting car to take them to their accommodation. Jai scanned the back of her body with his hands running them up and down the slinky fitting chintz garment and enjoying how she felt. As the driver got out of the car to open the back-door Jai stood behind Roxy slid his arms around her waist and pulled her close to him and softly kissed her neck; she melted onto his shoulder. Neither could wait to get back to their room.

Feedback of the seminar was high and positive especially his responses to Roxy. The audience found them both sexy and tantalising and they wanted what they had. According to the promotions office the entire act should be continued on a regular basis. The sexual innuendos the double meanings, the provocation was an enormous success with the entire audience. It aroused the audience and made them feel alive.

As time passed the seminars were all based on this format and as Roxy gained more confidence, she would do more platforms in the middle and let Jai do the main contents from beginning and then the finale maintaining the sexual inferences throughout the performance.

He added in the King Louis's story, explaining how he didn't know he was in love with her, but Roxy knew. "She didn't tell me. I'm not the brightest tool in the shed when it comes to love. Two bad marriages behind me; love was not my obvious forte, but she said I had to find out for myself. She had a heart incident and I thought I was going to lose her; I found out in a hurry that I loved her.

It took me awhile for me to get the courage I needed to return the love she had for me; without her heart seizure I would never have realised how much I loved her; but I couldn't let her go. Her family wanted to take her away up north and I couldn't bear to never see her again. That was the pressure I needed to stand up and do what I did.

I went into the hospital and I took her home, with me, and we've never been apart since.

"No, I didn't kidnap her," he pauses and laughs at the front seat audience, "she came with me, but we both wanted the same thing; my point is sometimes we need a brick to wake us up. My past life perceptions were preventing me from realising that my future would be different.

Full of surprises, all the time, full of surprises; We have had the most amazing life and I wouldn't change it for the world."

Jai learnt through Roxy how to use many anecdotes of their life together to create love and laughter in his audience and each time more people returned simply to experience their joy to take home with them.

CHAPTER 11

CREATING PERDITION

After twelve years on the road, it was suddenly over. Roxy had her final heart seizure. There was no coming back from this one. It was acute; there was no warning, and she died in Jai's arms, waiting for the ambulance. They couldn't revive her. He couldn't let her go.

Every cell in his body ached so heavily he didn't think he would survive. The tearing apart, the void, the darkness, and the loneliness was more wretched than he could bear. He tried not to shut her out this time; he knew this was important, but the unrelenting pain was crippling. He would go to the beach and talk but there was no answer, no reprieve. He felt she had left him and taken all their love with her. She was gone and so was their love, all he could feel was this endless torment rendering at is heart.

The stress, anxiety, aloneness was more than he could handle, so he decided to leave the bay. He told himself it would only be for a while. Everything reminded him of being without her. He would come back one day, but for now, he had to leave, he had to breathe again.

The evening before his departure, he went down to the bay; this would be the last time he would stand there. This pain was too unbearable. Her favourite music was belting down from the café as if it was punishing him. He heard the music and he fell to the ground crippled with pain, rocking himself inconsolably to find some solace, but it wasn't working.

"I'm trying, I'm trying" he screamed as his tears drenched his face and his gut cramped with pain. "Dear God Roxy what do you want me to do? Geez I loved you so much." He tried to stand up but fell again "Flamin' hell, I do l love you, I do, but ….this wretched pain. I can't get rid of it." He tried to stand again.

Out of nowhere came a huge gust of wind that literally picked him up and dumped him a metre away on the sand flat on his back. After a while he caught his breath. He sat up and dusted the sand off, "Thank you. I love you too' he sarcastically blubbered to himself in disgust.

After a pause, a realisation overwhelmed him. At first, he thought himself crazy then, "could it be? Is this how it works? Is it possible? Is it possible that Roxy answered me? He echoed the words again, "thank you, I love you too" He started laughing heartily; "Roxy" he yelled as he fell back on the sand "if that's you, if that's you, yes!" He let the sand flow through his fingers. He looked around him and became excited. The wind the water the sky all of it was telling him how much Roxy loved him and was still within him. She was here.

He rolled and kicked on the sand, lay on his back and yelled with extreme excitement. "Roxy Tagore; I love you," He lay there for a long while soaking up everything, absorbing everything for it all was Roxy. *He* had been rejecting it, but by absorbing it she was not only within him she was in everything around him as well. He finally got it. It was never her; she was only echoing him echoing the love within them both, within all of us. She was his reflection of THE LOVE. He was the disconnection, not her. He created a new heart rendering emotion and gave it a name. Wretchedness. Then he began to live his life through that new emotion of unrelenting pain. It was his choice. Yes, Roxy was no longer with him physically, but that love? That love is within him always. Their love is within him always. It's his no one can take that away from him. It is him. She is within him always.

He struggled to his feet and walked back up the path to his home. This new epiphany was mind boggling. His entire being had been torn apart at his perception of her loss. He felt his heart was bleeding and ripped apart and shredded, then his soul or something reawakened. A huge veil had been lifted. All his illusionary pain was gone and every painful part of his body has been replaced with this extraordinary feeling of high energy, ecstasy and happiness. Everything was not only going to be okay; it will be perfect. He decided to unpack his luggage and return to living. He sat at his desk and began instantly writing. This is how it works. He had just lived it. The entire act of our creativeness was before him, he had to write it down while the adrenalin was high.

The question Roxy asked; why would we choose the pain over the happiness? He wrote as he answered her puzzling question. The love is in everything. It's too is nothing but a choice. It has no memory; it simply is human perception like everything else. Until we activate it, it simply is. The fractal maths of it is in every miniscule cell of our body, zillions upon zillions of them, meaning the ability to create it, the information to create it is in every cell of our conscious body. Through my perception of the loss, I transferred the love to Roxy, to her smile, her touch, the happiness we shared and when she left it wasn't in front of me anymore. I believed she took our love with her.

Roxy you said you had a vivid imagination, well we all do. I altered the fractal information of our love into a fractal binary of intense loss, pain, anger, lack of control, stress and anxiety to name a few, I changed the fractal binary in my body and Karma personified my new mathematical equation and I wore it. I wore it inwardly and outwardly for three and a half months. I experienced nothing but pain. Every thought and feeling every day for three and a half months. But I was lucky; the overwhelming love within me, the love that my beautiful Roxy and I share every day we were together, revealed itself again to me and I found not only my love of Roxy again, but I found me again.

The equation of love is always there. It will always be there. It is the mathematical equation of the perfection of the entire universe. It is the basic algorithm of everything. It is our choice whether we want to use it or not. It is when you add programs to it or alter it, that you get lost; no, you don't get lost, you experience an alternative lifestyle. I unintentionally added victim to the equation and started living in full painful victim mode, I simply had to delete my new program and return to my basic algorithm. I used to think this love was like the ocean, it is the Godness of the universe. It will exist whether I use it or not, and that was the law of separation. When we alter the basic fractal maths and adjust it to another formulation then have to exist through that new persona. It always comes back to our creation of loss of power. We then create other emotions to compensate for our void. They get out of control creating addictions to inform us we are out of control.

I was out of control. I was terribly alone and I was running away. The victimisation was physically weighing me down I had to get out from under. I created all of that. I used the transference of allegiance and gave our love a name "Roxy."

The love of the universe is neutral, it is there whether you use it or not; but life is certainly much sweeter when you want to use it. Roxy isn't the love, I'm not the love but if I choose it, it will exist within every component of my being and with my creative imagination and karma's, the person I now create will be extensively happy, joyous and be able to live with the beautiful memory of the love shared with my beautiful Roxy. I can create this. There are no rules. I can create the love I want to have. I can live the love I want to exist with.

I can believe that through our love Roxy is still with me in and through everything. I create through my perception the love I want. Karma will personify that love through me. I will wear that love in everything I do and say and it will exist through me and my life.

I will continue our work because as Roxy says' we owe it to all those who are following us to be the happiest we can be. Some of their paths are arduous and we have already travelled them. We cannot do it for them, but we can make their endgame and future paths worthwhile.

For the first time in weeks Jai went to sleep that night peacefully. The spirit of new revelation let him imagine Roxy lay beside him.

Next morning Jai went to the cafe and all were surprised to see him. "Change of plans," he smiled.

Jason had to agree. He wasn't his usual happy self. It appeared Val was contesting the will and laying claim to the café. Jai felt this was serious. The bay could lose the café.

Jai went home and decided to go the lawyer. He had no idea what he could do but he would find out about Val's chances to ruin Roxy's dream for the café to stay in the Bay.

Sitting in a comfortable chair in the lawyer's office, he wanted to know how she could contest this document. His argument was he was married to Roxy if anyone owned it, he should. However, there were technicalities in that argument. There was no paper work to be found stating that Roxy actually and legally gave Jason the restaurant. Jai owned the café and Val could contest because there was no pre-nup and Roxy owned it before they were married but the final decision would belong to the justice system as the restaurant is not in Roxy's will. Jai paced up and down in the office, in his head he pleaded, "Roxy I need your help."

"How much is the café worth?" He asked the lawyer.

"It is a considerable amount but she wants $300,000," was the response. "It's officially worth far more than that but she wants her share,"

"So, Val wants $300000, that's what this is about; the money." pounced Jai. The lawyer, "Her argument is, you married her for her property and assets, yes, and in her state, she is allowed to contest it."

He paced some more. "Okay," thought Jai, "I'll pay her $300000. I'll bring you a cheque and you can give it to her saying it was sold. You don't have to tell her to whom."

"Then the official deed to the property would have to be placed in your hands" was the lawyer's response

"No," said Jai "the deed is to be signed over to Jason and Jonah; that was Roxy's wish."

"Later, but for now let's execute our plan of action," explained the lawyer. They went through more details of how to handle this sensitive situation; then Jai phoned his bank to make arrangements and as soon as the cheque was ready, he picked it up and gave it to the lawyer. "Make her sign for it." Then he left. Roxy's little rental house would cover most of that expense so now he would sell it and allow all past debts to be admonished.

He went to the beach. "Now all past debts are paid Roxy; we're clear." He remembered Roxy's past with her sister and Alex. "Now the financial debts are finished." Jai believed, for some reason this debt, this money had to be re-paid. Now there is no connection to anyone trying to steal from us again."

This act of victimisation had a purpose, Jai respected that and refused to become a victim to it. He allowed Val to have what she deemed she deserved. Now that was her path, right or wrong, it was hers and hers alone. Both he and Roxy allowed her to walk it.

His enthusiasm for life now became vibrant again and he couldn't wait to complete on his new book.

"Perceptional Joy; You have a choice." this would be their love story and how she is still all around him every second of the day through the love he created. He now knew how the unconditional love of true soul mates over comes all odds even death. She was still with him in absolutely everything around him. The love of his universe bound them together, she shared the love in all things around him, the wind, the sand, the water, and all he had to do was ask and a breeze would flow through his hair and around him.

It felt like Roxy was using the elements of this dimension to show him she was still here. It was like a babushka doll; world within worlds. They couldn't see each other's world but they could communicate through the love they both shared in every dimension.

The book flowed; it was easy to write. There was no more overcrowding of information. As he wrote about their love; the adoration of his wife's persistence to save and reunite them exuded through every word. Remembering all the amazing moments they had created for both of them to move into in their future life radiated on every page. As Rumi said, 'what you are looking for is looking for you.' "Of course, it is," he responded, "because I am now open to receiving it."

After 65 days a manuscript was taking shape. He re-edited it and was extremely happy with the results. This would probably be the best he has ever done. Now it was up to his publisher and editor to knock out the bloopers.

He was back to his old self again, no he was better than his old self. His old routine of a good swim and run of a morning followed by some light weight exercises. He would then go to the café, and grab his chai. Occasionally Gary would call him in for assistance at the studio. His life was taking another path and he was enjoying himself. Life was better than ever before, he made sure of that.

Jesse came to him and told him Frank was looking for him and it sounded urgent. The last time he had words with Frank was about twelve years ago when that man was hit by the car and he came to interrogate him. When he turns up it is never good news. "What does he want?"

"He's at the studio" confirmed Jesse anxiously.

"Okay I'm coming." Jai collected his gear, finished his drink, waved to Jason and walked to the studio just down the road.

Frank was never a happy gent and he was his usual repressive self today. Jai walked in and place his gear behind the door.

"You took your sweet time," grunted Frank.

"Nice to see you too Frank." Gary came in with a coffee. "You might need this."

Jai looked at Frank "What's this about?"

"I'll get to that in a minute. When was the last time you heard from Alex Brodwin," queried Frank in his stoic interrogating voice?

"Alex, why what's happen to Alex?"

"Just answer the question," Frank interrupted.

Jai had to think. "I haven't seen him since before I married Roxy. He didn't respond to our request to come to the wedding. That would be nearly over twelve and half years ago. I thought he moved."

"You didn't think there might be something wrong?" queried Frank

"No, I was living my life with Roxy. I didn't require his services. He worked at Multi Level Promotions. I wasn't his only client. Now what's going on?"

"You friend was found at the bottom of the bay," responded Frank with his over cocky attitude .

"I put some scotch in it dad" whispered Gary, referring to the coffee.

Jai just sat there stunned. "Wha! Who would want to hurt Alex?"

"That's what we want to know? Do you know where he has been the last few years?"

"No idea really. He left suddenly years ago and I haven't heard anything. He did say the last time I saw him that he would be up north and if I wanted him to contact his office. He handed my contract to three consultants at his office and they were good so I never went any further," reacted Jai still trying to fathom what he just heard.

"Why did he have this information in his car?"

He handed him some advertising information about his book. 'That's my book. I've got no idea."

"No premonitions?" said Frank sarcastically. They exchange caustic glances. "Do you have his number? We never found his phone?" declared Frank astutely.

Jai went to retrieve his business card, but Gary responded more quickly and went to the desk file carrier and pulled out Alex's card. He then handed it to the inspector.

"That's over twelve years old," responded Jai believing it to be extremely out of date.

Frank rose to his feet, thanked Gary for the coffee and started walking out. As he went out, he saw a promotional poster on the wall referencing Jai and Roxy at one of their last seminars.

"You know my wife spent $200 of my money to go see one of your fancy dancy things and now she's trying to change everything. You need to stay out of people's good marriages."

Jai had finally encountered enough insults for this man, he stood up and faced Frank in frustration, "If you missus came to one of my seminars, she's not so happy and she's looking for more. Maybe she wants more than your money Frank. Maybe she wants more than your job and your crap attitude Frank. For some bloody reason that woman loves you Frank and she wants *you*, not you now; the you she knew, the you she fell in love with Frank. Personally, I think she's on a lost cause, but she willing to fight for you Frank. She thinks you are worth it."

Jai turned to walk away then briskly turned back, "and for the record Frank that little piece of counselling costs around $200 so that should make us even"

Frank stormed out and slammed the door.

"What the hell dad?" barfed Gary.

"That guy has been a pain in my arse since we went to school. He joined the cops to pursue his, *bullying* career. Vicky his wife; what that woman sees in him has got me beat. She has idolised him from the beginning. He has an absolute treasure there and he really doesn't deserve her but that woman adores him." He stopped talking for a while then mumbled as he grinned, "you have no idea how good that felt. He can't stand the fact that I enjoy my job and he hates his," he continued laughing.

Jesse looked at him sarcastically, "oh you told him," he sniggered.

"Oh, shut up" curse Jai as both of them laughed, realising that his rebuttal would have consequences. They both continued laughing.

Jai was in a room surrounded by loving people, but he felt so terribly alone. This is not something one assumes will take place in one's life. He then recalled Roxy's statement how these types of people referring to Alex, cruise through life hurting others unscathed and not responsible for their actions.

"Apparently these people do meet their destiny in one form or another, my lovely." Then all of a sudden reality hit again, "Murder?" He questioned, "Murder" he repeated trying to absorb the information. I suppose I should have seen it coming. He did have some very jagged past lives. He sipped the coffee as he rubbed his forehead and then a client turned up. "I'd better go."

"No dad" pleaded Gary, "don't be alone today; stay here and do some paper work or something and I'll take you home later; actually, you can stay with us for a few days if you like."

"I'll be right son, but thanks, may be later." Jai retrieved his jacket and gear, blew a kiss to his lovely lady hanging on the wall and quietly left as Gary attended to his client.

Jesse followed him out to ensure his friend was okay. Jai patted him on the back and reassured him he was fine and continued on his way home. Jesse stood and watched as his friend drove into the nothingness.

"What a day!" Jai sat at his desk and sighed at all the events that have taken place over the last ten years, now this. "Who the hell did Alex cross? How did he end up in the drink?"

Jai's concentration was frazzled due to the news he received. He had no idea how to handle it. It was given to him for a reason. He and Alex shared many an existence together in the past. For Alex to end up in a murder dimension he would have had to have created an emotion for it to perform through him. Something drew him to the town where all this took place.

Strange how that took place, he just up and left. Whatever it was it was really strong. "Now," he thought, " I have to release all the information and allow it to be Alex's journey alone, not mine. What was Roxy's story about the Guru," he had to laugh. "Don't ask! Laugh and don't ask." Then he relaxed and remembered her story.

WHAT IS NIRVANA?

The student asks his Guru "What is Nirvana?"
His teacher responds "Whatever you perceive it to be."
"But master once you perceive something it becomes that perception." Answers the student quite perplexed.
"That is true,' answered his guru.
"If Nirvana is simply my perception of what I think it is, then where do you go when you meditate?"
His master starts laughing "nowhere," his master continues laughing and laughing
This perplexes the student even more . "Why do you laugh Master?" he queries.
"What's your next question?" Laughs the guru.
The student had to think about it "what's nowhere?"
"Now you have asked. Now through your perception it is somewhere." He laughs.
"But I'm still confused master."
"Don't ask my son; don't ask." His master vanished.
Many years passed and this quandary still puzzled the student.
Then the spark of Nirvana struck him.
You already have everything you want and need. You create it all.
He laughed as he understood. Nirvana means; "don't ask!"

CHAPTER 12

FORGING THE PATH

Several weeks passed and rumours swathed the bay as to Alex's demise. Jai's book was starting to hit the shelves and was receiving extraordinary accolades. It was time to prepare for the next step of his promotion, however there were several impasses.

Jai walked down to his favourite part of the bay and sat on the retaining wall; he soaked up the sun and talked to his Roxy. He'd been relaxing quite comfortably for several minutes when Jesse came to join him.

"Heard the latest?" exploded Jesse in reference to Alex. Jai shook his head and beckoned no. "They found his ex-wife in some scrub up north as well. They were both under fake names."

"What?" questioned jai as he frowned in exasperation. "What next?"

"Oh, there's more" said Jesse slavering at the mouth with each salacious morsel he was about to share. "Long story or short; Alex ran away with his ex from her ex mob husband. Apparently, he used to bash her around a bit, so Alex rescued her about six years ago. They went into hiding. The big boss had two of his yobbos deal with both of them. They found his phone."

"What a mess!" responded an astounded Jai? "Sounds like some soap opera." He sniggered as he says "The only time Alex saved anyone's life and it gets him killed. Where's the irony in that?"

There was a lull in the conversation then "Hey your books a success, number three this week that's got to be good hasn't it?"

Jai smiled at his friend's quickly change of subject.

"Kinky ending though," frowned his friend as he shook his head.

Jai had to giggle as he meant the ending of his book to bring hope to everyone about their final place of peace. "Not really," Jai went deep into thought "I've got to be the only person I know who is looking forward to the day he dies," he laughed.

"Roxy had it wrong you know. You don't die and go somewhere and you don't take the love with you. You become the love when you create it and from that love you get everything you ask for, same as every other emotion you simply choose love. It's all around you and they are an enormous part of it. She used to say I had to plant the flower in women so they could rise above the dimension and bring men up to join them as one. But she was wrong.

I've learnt more from her since she passed than what she told me while she was alive." He paused and reminisced. Jesse listened to his friends new theories and smiled as he now believed his friend finally understood what he himself had been teaching for years.

" I've personally felt that tearing of the yin yang heart and the healing. Every person already has the blossom in them, it's in their imagination. Yeah and as men and women we have buried it down under thousands even millions of years of abuse, but I don't have to replant a new seed, I simply have to awaken the one that is already within them and show them how to fertilise it. They need to learn how to empower their creative imagination to use other emotions. Once they do, the same laws will apply. It's the outcome that will differ. Both male and female will be unstoppable."

"You should have written that in your book" responded Jesse as he patted his friend on the back.

"The next one," nodded Jai. Jesse got up to leave, said his goodbyes and as he wandered up the hill he shouted; "Hey did you know old Frank resigned?"

"No, but now I've got bigger fish to fry." He started to leave and quietly mumbled to himself. "Now I need to find a new promotions manager. With Alex gone the company will fold. Alex was the best in his business I have no idea where I'll get one as good now."

The Prophet

Jai headed down to the Waterfront Café. Jason greeted him with a huge "thank you."

Jai was a little bewildered.

Jason continued; "you; you and Roxy; I read your book; you both gave me the café. I had no idea why her daughter stopped with the contesting of the will. Thanks to your vote of confidence, it means a lot to us. I've got so many new plans with new savouries and cakes to introduce, my head is exploding. You said she is still with us; do you really believe it, cos sometimes I think she's tells me what cakes to introduce; it's really crazy."

"Oh yeah, I really believe it" as he pointed to a zucchini slice to have with his chai.

Jason continued, "That reminds me a guy in came looking for you. He left his card. Here it is. He does some kind of media promotions."

Jai laughed to himself; unbelievable, he thought. Sometimes, even the crazy is crazy. "thank you," and he took the card.

He sat at his regular table and pulled out his phone. He dialled the number on the card. They had a small chat, Jai informed him of his location and his new promotional officer joined him for a coffee and a chat.

As he looked up at the door, he saw Frank and his wife. He was holding her hand and he look relaxed and happy. Jai gave a giggle, "even him; my god Roxy is no one out of bounds; now that one is a miracle."

Jai and the promotions manager hit it off really well. He had brilliant contacts not only local but interstate. He wanted to take Jai state-wide. There was nothing holding him here so he went for it. It will be physically exhausting so he needed to be fit.

Jai upped his training and started eating healthily again. The tour was prepared for 6 weeks covering several small and two major towns. Tickets went on sale through major ticket sale holders. All that needed to be done was Jai's power point and his performance.

He knew what he wanted to say but "Perceptional Joy" is a very sensitive subject and it had to be handled with thoughtfulness, intelligence and respect. You could lose an audience very easily on aspects that very personal. This one was about our personal recovery after serious loss. He had spoken on this subject before but this time, he had personally experienced it and recovered, fully.

His orations would take an hour and a half with a 20-minute break.

If this tour is successful, then an offer had been welcomed for him to platform with other celebrities on future weekend getaways. This would be big time and a lot of fun; so, there was a lot hanging on this tour's success. It would be the first time without Roxy. It had been a while since he did solo, but he would be talking about her.

When he spoke about her there was an overwhelming feeling love and comfort within him. A feeling saying "This is Us;" He could work from that. He now fully grasped the solo flight when you release all victimisation or the crutch. He understood why we chose the other path.

Although Einstein said, walking with the crowd you stay with the crowd and walking alone opens amazing doors beyond your highest expectations; what he didn't say was being the solo tree in the middle of a field although magnificently beautiful it is still alone, and maybe sometimes that is too painful.

But what if you filled that tree with unbelievable love. What if you create your world filled with amazing love and you surrounded yourself with a forest of trees just like yourself. You would all be free to be, yet joined in amazing creativeness. That's what we truly want.

13
CHAPTER

PERCEPTIONAL JOY

Jai started his tour on familiar ground. This first seminar would assess the glitches, and then he would hit the road, 45 days of touring; bad food, lack of sleep and hard work. He had a bus and a tour group. These people would set up the stages and the video tapings. They would also set up his power point. They then cleaned it all up. He simply has to perform and entertain. He never thought of it as entertainment; however, this was a different league. He was a highly paid performer, and many were dependent on his success.

This set up was completely different from the small promos Alex and his company did. He still sold his books videos and tapes on site, however with this group the videos were in front of the crowd at the new venue the next day streamed worldwide on the web.

The auditorium was full. It had four aisles, two on the extreme outside and two in the centre. The entire sound system, including Jai's computer, all connected to and were controlled from the media system in the centre of the hall.

All Jai had to do was talk. He had an earphone instructing him of all the comings and goings throughout the night; when his power point changed; when quotes were required; when breaks were required; and lighting; everything was computerised and programmed.

They even kept him on track with his oration.

Loud exhilarating pumping music plays throughout the auditorium as the audience enters and take their seats. When the theatre is over two thirds full, an emcee stands in front of the crowd compelling them to clap and sing along, exciting them and raising the high energy within the room.

Once the theatre has reached a full capacity, the emcee takes the centre stage and starts introducing tonight's guest of honour in a loud salesperson's voice. "He's a multiple author who has been writing for over twenty years; He is introducing his latest book, "Perceptional Joy." He is a highly qualified hypnotherapist with a huge array of tapes, videos to assist with smoking, career, weight loss and anything that ails you. His studio releases meditation tapes, courses for higher relaxation and higher spirituality. He has behind him numerous seminars and learning programs on the reincarnation continuum. So, here and now on centre stage let's give a warm huge welcome to Jaaai Tagore."

The emcee walks backward off the stage clapping madly as the audience stands up and applauds excitedly. Jai make his entrance waving both his hands in anticipation. His head was in awe at the excitement within the audience. He was filled with eagerness himself as he thought "this is crazy."

He let the audience calm down and take their seats and waited till the din died, then spoke with a normal voice to welcome his fantastic audience and pointed out the program's highlights including breaks. He didn't have to strain his voice in any way as the audio system monitored the loudness through the sound system.

He breathed a sigh and began." Thank you so much. This is my first solo seminar in a long time. My beautiful Roxy passed away several months ago and this get together is about our journey and my journey back from her loss. As was pointed out in my intro, my new book in on sale and usually a seminar is an abridged version of each publication but my objective this time is to give a more comprehensive version for you to take with you to enhance your reading experience. I still research reincarnation continuum, it explains more to me than any other form of teaching so it is more of an addiction as opposed to research. My frame of mind is continuously dictating from that threshold. It is second nature and natural to me now.

In my previous books I've pointed out how the long-term historical struggle of subservience and victimisation has served with minor races, sexes, along with flora and fauna throughout the world over 70000 years dating back to Egyptian times and before.

In my latest book I have catechized how the teachings of Genesis are actually not any form of teachings of a god but are historical creations of a narcissistic domineering supremist male king who created a law and then proclaimed it to be of a god. He then enforced that law and that is how we as a world still maintain his allegiances today and from that perspective keep creating more blinding victimisation for us to experience. Now some may disagree and some may agree that is irrelevant, I am not here to tell you to alter your religious beliefs, what is important is how we improve what we have and how to get it now, today.

The old canons have been proven to be historically incorrect. There are too many anomalies. The results show that by adhering to these old allegiances, we have or are going to actually destroy every living thing in existence; land, air, water, earth and metal and humans. These are the elements of our existence and man not woman, and man, simply man, has taken every element and abused every single one of them to near extinction. This is not the plan of any god; this is the plan of the greedy narcissistic male syndrome or emotion, but I'll do more on that later.

Now before I progress any further let me clarify the male narcissistic path. We have all walked it at one time or another; both male and female. So, although the path is male dominance, we all at one time, chose to partake of that path, why because we wanted to control our pain;" he paused, then continued. "Through emotional reaction."

I have two grandsons, great kids, and they love smash up derby, especially if the ground has been wet. So, do I and I'll take them whenever it is in town. But that environment is contained and controlled. There are fire brigades, ambulances and many other security people to ensure that the entertainment is no more than that.

Outside the arena, this same action is taking place and it is not contained, it is very insecure and it can in some places be extremely dangerous. It is out of control, so are we." He again paused. This was going to be harder than expected. He missed the banter between he and his lovely wife.

"The people in charge of our outside world have no aims of stopping it and will engage in more over and over again and they have no intentions of relenting. When a group or a leader tries, they are usually suppressed, until we return to this constant disorder or worse.

I'm not condemning men as such either. Men have been unjustifiably abused as well by their own gender. This is Darwin's theory of evolution with white supremacy over all beings. But he didn't invent the genre. This mad half cut attitude was already present, he simply recognised and diagnosed it. He didn't cure it either, he gave it to the supremist who then took it and ran with it; not to save the world but to enhance their own worlds for personal power and wealth. What that theory has done now is created more segregation between all genres.

The most dominant will survive, all the rest will serve. This sounds a bit like a female's movement for equality, but it really isn't. I'm hoping it will be a means to so much more. We are all paving this path and there is a really sad reason, but we can fix it. You won't stop what is happening in the world but you can repair what is happening in YOUR world. That's all you can do. You can only alter *your* world, and let *the* world play by its own curriculum.

Philosophically this separation started with the old dogma. It is written in the bible which originates from the Edict of Milan by Constantine in 364AD. It dictates that man is created in the same image as god. However, woman was created from the lower specimen of man through his rib and so forth all other formations of life are here to serve man, and he is to take care of them; well he's doing a lousy job." There was scattered applauding in the audience. He laughed.

"Thank you, I wasn't expecting that."

"Metaphysically what this synopsis actually looks like is all in paradise was equal and happy; male female animals, plants land, and water; all protected and created from and in accordance with, and here is the key, no emotions existed until man created them. They created them out of responses to their environment. You want proof. The universe, god, the cosmos, is completely unemotional, it is the "I AM." That's it nothing more. However, from the "I AM" we have the capacity to create absolutely everything we want and don't want for that matter.

Man and woman were united as one along with all existence. When in a state of nothingness, you are limitless. That's what the nothingness does for you. It's the magic wand of the universe. It's Nirvana. You then have to ask, what went wrong? Nothing went wrong; man, simply asked.

When you ask, an emotion is created. From that emotion karma translates that information into your DNA. Your DNA attaches it to every individual cell in your body and there are zillions, you now personify that emotion physically, spiritually and mentally, and the Law of Attraction magnetises more of the same emotion to you. You react again creating new emotion and the continuum recommences, on and on and on. Now the glitch. Once you are personified, every word you speak is your bible. So, if you abuse another human being in your first life, your DNA personifies that information; in your body you die and return to become that abused person in your next life. That is the reincarnation component of the continuum. When you react again, you will return to your new emotional reaction and that's how they work together. It's a spiral that keeps rolling forward getting bigger every time.

His jitters were subsiding now. He smiles and starts his entertaining, "According to the biblical story, a woman was the instigator of all the trouble." He smiles and points to some women in the audience. "But the evidence of history disclaims that version of events." He winks and says "saved" then he pauses and laughs. "History displays that supremist man not only separated from woman, he separated himself from every other form of life. He then made her the scape goat and all other objects his slave. Now I say supremist because there are some races who see themselves above all other life forms on earth. However, there are some aboriginals and natives who see life on earth as one with them but still treat women as slaves or lower. My point is although there are races who respect the earth and its life forms, there appears throughout history to be little record of equality or acceptance of woman as equivalence to men. Even when Elizabeth the first ruled it was under male decrees. The minute she married she lost everything to the male. The reigning queen now had to hand over her power to a government. Victoria is probably the only who told them to bugger off, but even she had difficulties. That's simply history. Back to the garden.

What the reincarnation continuum suggests is in his next life, he then became the female product of his own abuse. Now in female form he then rejects the abuse creating in her next life the same maltreatment again out of revenge. From there we then portrayed the worst case of narcissistic abuse and destruction on all of life to almost extinction. There is a quote that states "if a narcissist cannot control you, they will control how others perceive you."

Throughout history, the defamation against the recipient as female and lessor units has been exactly that, lies, betrayal, denigration and subservience, so from this position woman was never able to stand her own ground. Even Madame Pompadour supplied her king with virgins only then to turn them into street workers struggling to survive.

The male concept wasn't men only it is the power of the sovereignty. However, in all cases, we were victims of our own creativeness. Roxy's dream was to empower women again. She became empowered after an arduous path and as she says 'if she can do it and have the most amazing life, she wanted that for all women.

How did she do that? She altered her perception. But to do that she had to learn what to alter. So, let's alter histories scenario.

Let's suppose man screwed up in the Garden of Eden and let's then try to imagine another scenario. He separated from woman, creating the yin/yang. As one being, he would now be oppressor and recipient. As oppressor he became independent, strong. He assumed himself better than his recipient and everything else, so he divided all things into a duality of division. Them against him. He tore the oneness of self in half. He not only assumed himself to be in god's image and likeness, he assumed himself to be god.

From that time on he has created from his ego and as a result has only been able to create material things because by shattering the oneness, he doesn't believe he has any real magic; so, he has to do it physically. This is his own personal belief. However, he still has the capacity to think big, but he requires his lower recipients to do it for him by imprisoning him /her into slavery. This is his form of equality. Everyone working together to empower his ego.

Now you think that was thousands of years ago, but it wasn't. Only last century, Hitler who created his own bank because after WW1 he needed money to rebuild his starving Germany, then in 1939 with the help of Himmler they employed his SS to infiltrate a radio station in Germany, then claimed it to be an act of war by Poland giving them the right to invade Poland steal their property, their wealth and all the people. He then through slave labour forcing the Poles and Slavs to rebuild his Germany and his new army machines. Stalin did the same. It's occurring all around the world daily; we are simply closing our eyes to the facts.

Back to history; from that time on they created a god like themselves and by using this god as the rule of establishment they were able to use bullying tactics to fulfil the emptiness the only way they knew how.

The reason I'm advocating most of this part of the program with female bias is to illuminate why we are where we are. The second reason is if we keep going this way, this patriarchal regime has the capacity to destroy the human race and all living species into extinction.

The bottom line is, this path is simply not good enough. As a patriarchal regime it has shown us what we are capable of as a race and the results are before us. As a patriarchal race of oppressor versus recipients neither has the capacity to redeem the damage we have done. We obviously cannot have true equality under this regime. This slavery versus supremist is the only equality we will get.

Jai altered the subject now; "Lets' up the ante. My beautiful wife and soul mate passed away several months ago and you wonder why such a path would be chosen by us. We should be able to live out our lives together for ever. But my beautiful Roxy was always a brilliant teacher and this lesson revealed to me the entire truth and it helped me realise the intense extent we have suffered and why we insist on suffering even more.

Our love was unconditional. It was oneness in every sense of the word because of our work and the way we both expressed ourselves, we were always in accordance. For someone like me to find someone who was on the same brainwave as me proves there is someone for everyone." He gave a quirky look and grinned with the audience.

"When she passed my entire body split in two. It was as if a saw had cut me in half. The parting; the separation; the loss of her heart beat with mine was excruciating. I couldn't breathe; I couldn't work; I wanted out. My entire body was torn and shattered and I was emotionally bleeding. I could literally feel the rendering of my inner being. I wanted my Roxy back, but I thought that would never happen, could never happen.

As Rumi says -you have to break the heart to open the heart- I'm taking that one step further, to awaken the soul completely you have to destroy the unscrupulous narcissistic component of self. That is what I experienced.

The excruciating pain I was suffering at the loss of my soul mate was what I created out of my reaction to my lack of power and control over her death.

I deliberately maintained that emotion to keep reminding me that I had not only lost her but I couldn't prevent it and I wanted her back. The extenuating pain that I believed occurred to me when I lost Roxy is the horrendous pain, I created to divided me from me. I altered my perception. I began asking all forms of reactionary questions. From the questioning I created further ongoing emotional reactionary pain to experience over the next few months.

From that time on, I tried to cover up the pain by wanting superficial things outside myself. I wanted to run away and start somewhere else with new stuff; all those man-made material aspirations that are a means of trying to hide our pain. Food, money, power, war, genocide, impoverishment, drugs, all are a means to hide our powerlessness within us. I did the same. I substituted my pain I caused me by filling the void, I created inside of me, with stuff.

People use religion and the Jesus theory to save their souls, and they are using a man named Jesus to be their soul mate, but again this is the transference of allegiances. This is when you give your personal power away to an imaginary friend. If that helps them achieve their happiness then go for it. But long term it is still the giving away of your personal power and creating a crutch. As he is supposed to have said you go through him to get to god. Well if God is in every cell of your body and you don't know how to acquire love from that inner nothingness inside you, then use his name. The vibration of his name will heal you. You are still creating from the same love you have simply given it another name. That is allowed. There are no rules. If you want to create from that perception and it fulfills you, then do it. It doesn't matter what name you put on it, the name doesn't exist it is what you create within you," he paused then stressed, "that is what is important."

The Prophet

He continued as he now sat on his stool in the centre of the stage. "After weeks of horrendous pain, one evening when I would have been at the nadir of my emotional pain; I pleaded for Roxy to help me." he said sadly. " I screamed at her or someone to help me; then from nowhere this huge wind threw me about four meters back onto the sand. To say I was shaken would be an understatement. Coincidence? Probably. Weird? Most definitely," he grinned and paused, collecting his memories.

Then this overwhelming feeling of unbelievable love filled every particle of me. It took a while for me to formulate what had happened but I had just gone through one of the biggest transformations I would ever experience. Whether it was the knock on the head, I don't know.

Dramatic yes, and yes you do have to think weird to appreciate it and I fit both those categories, but when I finally absorbed all that occurred, I discovered the love I shared with Roxy was answering the biggest question of all time for me and I hope you as well.

The extenuating pain that occurred when I lost Roxy is an emotion, I created to remind me that we were divided. I didn't know that. Is it the same in every existence? I assumed the oppressor acted that way because he was a mean son of a gun. But if man, out of reaction to his pain, blamed her for all his pain, he would have reacted oppressively. She on the other hand in the same situation would have blamed him and reacted oppressively as well. She may have been the recipient but she used exactly the same reactionary emotions as her oppressor becoming one with him, thus, reincarnating to act and be like him in her next life.

From that time on we have been trying to cover up the pain with superficial things. I wanted to run away and start somewhere else with new stuff; all those man-made material aspirations that are a means of trying to hide our pain. This is all part of our creative questioning.

All this cold empty material outside stuff is informing us of what we are creating. They are all a means to hide from our emotional intent and banish the pain we caused by ignoring the one thing that will save us. I too was in full brunt victim mode. I was over indulging it and it was exacerbating my situation. I had a choice, victim or victor?

"Oh, I can make this weirder." He smirks at the audience and they laugh. "The name I gave my imaginary friend was Roxy she was my transference of Allegiance. However, in my perception now I like to believe it was the joined love of Roxy and me that we created while she was alive that reconnected with me on that beach. I imagine her dimension and this dimension connected through our love, like a bubble within a bubble. I felt and still always feel her around me every single moment of the day. Now although I cannot see her, I feel she is with me all the time because I keep reinventing the love we shared.

Now I'm really lucky because I know what my lovely Rose looked like. I know the curve of her face the smell of her hair the touch of her body, I've seen mine; but some of you haven't and that is what Roxy is telling me now. It is not how they look that reconnects you; it's the unbelievable unconditional love that connects you. By reconnecting to that love instead of going through the eternal maze of destruction, you fly over the top of the labyrinth strait to your soul mate and to the original source of the god loving unconditional love of the universe.

You can connect to your inner bubble.

Wow that was even poetic for me!" His audience reacts happily. "My Byron is showing." His audience laughed.

He needed that, he felt he was becoming a bit too intense.

"Every dimension and in all dimensions for that matter is a specific emotional energy that is used to create each painful dimension. For example, you may be a warrior so your dimension uses the emotional energies of war orientation.

A drug dimension utilises all the energies of that drug dimension. A violent murdering mafia dimension has the tools of that dimension to be used. For you to be attracted to each dimension you too have to have matching emotional energies. In today's age we can call them binaries. Your binary has to compute with the dimension you enter.

In one of your existence you will utilise the tools of your dimension in a very negative hateful manner. Therefore, for you to balance you as a person you will then have to return to the same dimension but this time you have to use the exact same tools as the recipient as your source. The tools of the dimension are simply tools; you are the motivational force behind the tool. Your questioning of how when where or why that tool is implemented attracts you to the dimension. You create the question, and you created the answer then you have to live it.

Little bit too deep? There are a few nods in the front here; it will become clearer as I continue. Like all things it will unfold and all will be revealed," he says dramatically.

He is travelling around the stage, down the stairs, and through the audience as he speaks.

"What we have to ask is; we are all responsible for the outcomes of this planet, so this separation, this division of oppressor /recipient has two sides to the story. Do you want to know?

The stronger the human, the more he keeps achieving through violence bullying and supercilious ego. Women who are defined weaker or recipient fight back, however in fighting back they are empowering the oppressive behaviour within themselves, thus becoming the oppressor in their next existence, got it?

What my objective today is to teach you how to return to your original self which is neutral, neither oppressor nor recipient. Teach you how to create the love you wish to embark on. Raise yourself higher than the conundrums surrounding you. Reconnect you to your soulmate and start working on the love you want to create so you can have the most exhilarating lives.

That's our plan of action.

This places you higher than narcissistic man, and once you are up there" he pauses and waits for silence, "stand your ground. Create a soul mate who will want to join you equally. You will be tested. Others *will* want you to rebel against your personal regime and fight for your rights, no! No fighting." He lingered. "You must not lower your tactics; you must remember what you truly and really want to achieve and why; for if you do, you will fall lower than you were before."

He wanders around the audience, "for example the traits of a narcissistic husband or lover will treat you with contempt but you being in victim mode apologise for them. He/she leaves you, and then wants to return to you; you accept. When they return, they treat you even worse than before and so it continues until you leave for good.

Even better example; this is one of Roxy's; this one is about the weight issue. The self-narcissist will allow you to lose weight, you will look great then it will not have you not only return to your old weight but you will gain an extra 20 kilo's why? Because you got rid of your narcissist emotion of imprisonment and then you let it return, so it returns and places you further down so you cannot get up again. You are in victim mode.

That's their rules; so, change them; become the person that you truly want to be and then you won't attract narcissists to you, even within you.

Easier said than done; unfortunately, that is true. Men don't know it but this is what they want too. Their problem is they are caught up in the digressiveness of the worlds around them, they don't know how to stop it.

We react to situations; thus, creating more of the situations for us to experience. We all have to rise above it and at this stage only women can and want to do that. From there they will raise the rest of the planet. Why does it have to happen this way? Because women are love; want to be loved and by being love and becoming love, they can attract to them their soul mate and re-join forces with them to create a better more loving planet. Men just don't do that, have you noticed?

He smiles at his audience, "does that give me extra brownie points" He does a power punch "Oh yeah!" He laughs as he walks back on stage "Let's continue. As women, they usually only choose abuse to retaliate, to explain the feeling of pain within them and they really don't want to abuse others, they want to love. They love the love thing really." He smiled. "That is who you are, admit it!" he asks. "And that is what you are made of."

Once women reconnect to the unconditional love of the universe, if you like, and start realising that this love is the love of the united soul partners, they will want that love for both their partner and themselves. They want it for their children, grandchildren family loved ones neighbours and the postman, they want to share it with everyone. They want to reconnect to their loved soul mate. They don't want to dominate with it by themselves. They want someone to share it with, someone to love and create with. And from experience, when they start creating, guys hang onto your socks.

Males love being independent; they normally don't want the unison. That's why they don't want to share. They feel they are losing themselves. The men who find their soul mates are totally different people to the average Joe blow. They want to be with their partners; they attract abundance on all forms; they shine happiness. They refrain from judgement and criticism. Their love for each other dictate's their lives. The heart lies. It is riddled with emotions and the biggest emotion is judgement and judgement forge their paths of destruction.

Many new age philosophies teach; you have to be there before you can walk it, and that is a true way of genuinely achieving. It is by relinquishing your victimised control that you receive the true self-empowered control. It is by recognising that, in giving away your power to any denigrating force, you then personify the victim force thus magnifying all avenues of that same victimising force to you.

By deliberately deciding not to be victim to anyone or anything because you recognise the future victimised paths it magnetises to you, you gain personal control. When you gain your personal control, you gain your self-empowerment. You have now opened the door to your amazing self-love and love unlimited. Like the swiss alp railway that was built years before the first train, you have to pave the way before you can walk it. You have to know where your path is going and let all your heart's desire come to you.

The path I'm putting forward for us all to cross today is the path to re-establish our contact with our inner soul then your soulmates. To re unite with that creative feeling of love, it reconnects us to the universal magic we deserve.

To do that you have to believe you have already found them. You have to daily walk the path of united love of you and your soul mate then that law of attraction will bring you together. Why? Because the law of attraction is attracted to your attachments. If your attachments are your soul mate and unconditional love it can only obey; it doesn't decide; the quandary may be that they are not here in this existence. Walk it anyway.

What I have since discovered since my wife departed is because I knew this path meant I had to love myself first. Now because I love Roxy and she in my imagination loves me. I double it. Now the truth is the actual love I'm feeling doesn't really exist, but my imagination doesn't know that and it lets me create whatever I want so, I created this love, then I doubled it." He laughs and winks at the audience. "Once you are free, there are no rules, no restriction, no limitations; the universe is yours to command. Just remember everything you command has cause and effect. So, make your effect as brilliant as your cause." he pauses and has a sip of drink and configures his thoughts again.

"Roxy knew she was ill and she would say 'I'm taking all the memories with me.' Any special memory of unbelievable love she would store to take with her, so we made millions of special memories.

Let me tell you about our path and believe me my soul mate and I walked a path similar to many of you through outrageous pettiness and pain but we created the pain to endure our loss of each other. Our journey was not an easy straight forward path. It was a violent, volatile, emotional maze that brought us together again; but it took us up to 1900 years or more to achieve it.

"We killed each other in two lives," he laughs with exasperation; and the audience responds. "What it did uncover was how we from our past life judgements then have to wear that history of that judgement as our garment. You change gender, religious beliefs, financial status, countries; we experienced a multitude of life experiences in a variety of ways.

Before I start explaining the paths of soul mates I would like to share with you a story my wife lovingly told me about a book she read many years ago called "The Magnificent Obsession" The main characters had fallen in love with the wife of a man who died because of his wealthy malevolence; but it was a star crossed love affair. She had lost her husband and her sight because of the hero. He decides to become a specialist physician. She on the other hand vanishes to some place to Mexico and slowly suffers.

He, in the book, meets a guru who teaches him the art of giving and receiving. The principle is when you assist someone who has a dream; you help them to achieve their dream that paves the path for your future direction. You never ask for the assistance to be returned it has to be passed forward to keep the path moving in an onward direction.

When this occurs the extent of their success reflects back on you, so the more you do, the more your inner happiness is achieved. To quote St Francis of Assisi; "It is in the giving that you receive" The hitch is also if you give it to a selfish greedy gluttonous person the energy of the gift implodes and all you receive is the emptiness of that gift.

The Prophet

In the story he assists a friend who wants to open a café. He gives him the money to start his dream at a university café and his friend is a huge success. In the friend's café there is a box at the end of the counter where he continues to assists young students to achieve their dreams and they return the money into a box and so that money will be used to help others.

In doing this act, the hero through an unbelievable miracle is reunited with his love under horrendous circumstances and he is able to save her life and her eye sight and achieve his ultimate dream.

My beautiful wife showed me that by being in the place of giving unconditional love to others we were able to achieve higher levels of happiness for ourselves.

Sharing your wealth is entirely your business; what will happen is you give to someone who has a magnificent dream; expect your highest dream to come true.

If money is required to achieve your dream, it will turn up for you and it will be more than you gave. As Roxy says -once you let the stuff fly you can't get rid of it. It just keeps coming back- as he giggles and "that is very true" the audience giggle also.

"That is the basis of this seminar. My objective is to give to you all, the most amazing gift of freedom to acquire the highest happiness you could ever receive. Money is not a gift, how you use it is. If you try to control money it will imprison you and inform you of your loss of empowerment; so free it and it will always come back to you.

With my beautiful wife and me, we had past life regressions, years apart but with the same hypnotherapist. Roxy recognised me in her regressions but I had no idea who she was. We had both physically altered in each journey, but Roxy informed me that it didn't matter what colour eyes I had, she was able to identify my soul every time.

When we started collaborating on different subjects, we would compare life times and we crossed paths many times. Roxy knew she was my soul mate long before I did, but she refused to inform me. She stated that I had to find out for myself. Because of past life dilemmas Roxy didn't want the same thing to occur this time so she kept quiet so our future lives would have a chance." He moved from his stool and continued his story.

"I'm so glad she didn't. Although our time together was shorter than I would have liked, our time together was the happiest I have ever experienced. She taught me more than I ever thought possible not so much about past life regression as much as she taught me about our real love and that, like a fingerprint we match perfectly. Once we find each other it's like a fire cracker on New Year's Eve. Hoo-hah!" he shakes his head.

"So first I'll let you go for your break an after the break we'll discuss the cataclysmic path we take over and over again to find each other."

Once the auditorium was emptied lighter softer music surrounded the theatre. Jai wasn't comfortable with the way things were proceeding. He had so much to say and wasn't confident that he could pull it off even though it was flowing smoothly.

He wanted both men and women to pick up the gauntlet realise they have a reason to be searching for a higher perspective in life. They were all on the right track and the reason, they were here at this seminar as a gender was because they had created a past that bought them here.

He needed to point out the body of history to demonstrate to them that they are physically carrying their trauma, its evolution, and as such they are deliberately attracting to them more of the same drama.

The motivating music started raging and the audience was returning and filling the seats. The lights dimmed as the stragglers re-entered. The screens came on and a huge image of Jai appeared on all three screens.

When the music stopped, he asked if all were happy with all things so far and, were they ready to take their final journey?" The audience applauded and let him start.

"To enter into the life paths, you have to understand how you decipher the punishment you have both endured and perpetrated.

This is male and female alike. Our past history is defined in our appearance. To understand your body, you have to understand your history. To decipher your history, you have to become an objective observer of your now.

Every person who has abused you, physically, mentally emotionally are informing you of your past personalities. Guys you may have experienced heart break, unhappiness, well this is informing you that this also is a past life experience.

Your body will define whether you are victim or perpetrator. Your armour will develop to the extent of the abuse. You will cover your heart with your body. This is a key mechanism to our evolution; the change in the heritable trait's, characteristic of a population over generations; the adaptation of this species to our pain and heartache. We are a dramatic lot." That quote broke the silence.

"As females they are prone to protect their sexual organs and their hearts, and their souls. When counselling people with obesity one strong issue that is dominant is the obesity and how lack of weight control starts at puberty.

The other obvious trait as I pointed out earlier is with many with weight challenges are once they lose the weight within a short period not only do, they put the weight back on they add an extra 20 kilos. This also is because of emotional narcissistic abuse, and *you* are your narcissist.

The narcissistic body tries to make the armour stronger so as not to allow penetration of future violence. The very core of the protection source has to be found. Many have not only been abused in this lifetime, but also in past lives as well. To overcome this, you have to realise you were also a perpetrator of the violence as well as a victim. You do not have to know the type of violence you had to endure; you only have to release the victimising relationship within you now. The people, places, things around you will inform you of what is imprisoning you. You will OVER REACT. Your emotion in your over reaction is informing you of what is victimising you. If someone in front of you is accusing you of not approving of their actions and you then inform others in an over reacting way, you have to realise you are using the very same emotional reaction that your nemesis was using. There is your victimising emotional obstacle. Allow your nemesis to have their opinion. You now know where they will end up and you now have the choice whether you wish to join them or not.

As I go through our past life dramas, imagine the types of armour created during each lifetime. Roxy's past life experience started one life time before we met. This continuance goes back further but for our soul mate experience this basically starts it.

My journey, in regards soul mate relationship has taken about 1900 years to reconnect and start again, now we will enjoy each other in eternal unconditional love. The reason I informing you of these is to open your eyes to not only reincarnation continuance, but how allegiances or false beliefs create purposes that forge our emotional attachment that create chaos for each lifetime.

The first part of this journey was when Roxy as a female was over looked in the inheritance of a huge property due to her gender. It was a law created to perpetrate means to ensure future materialistic wealth at the same time, denigrating women. Her younger brother, who was totally derelict in his lifestyle, inherited the entire estate. She had to marry well to survive. She fought back. The fighting started creating a strong body armour based on hatred, envy and jealousy. She created those emotions, those emotions then personified her.

After a period of time her brother had run the estate into ruin; Roxy and her husband bought the property for a pittance leaving the brother destitute. He died poor, lost, starving and forsaken. Roxy lived out her life in material wealth, power and judgement of the laws of the land. We agreed that her perceptions of the law's injustice created her hardening in her heart and it imprinted a karmic imbalance to take place in future lives.

Her next life was when we married. It was a Celtic wedding. I was betrothed to a daughter of a well to do Celtic landowner. I went into their house and kissed the wrong girl, and nearly started WW4.

Well it created a huge uproar; the father was going to kill me and my father was going to disinherit me," Jai was laughing at the mess he'd created. "Then this Celtic mother spoke up and my lord when she spoke there was silence.

The souls have spoken; it is done. Then she slammed down her staff on the floor and not another word was spoken. The wedding went ahead and however, her unhappy sister married a good neighbour of mine.

At our celebration we opted to do the soul mate ceremony to awaken our souls. Roxy and I actually achieved it, many didn't. Whether we were soul mates before the ceremony I don't know, but we were certainly soul mates after.

Our relationship was alive, loving and consumed with love. We had a small estate and were independent. Civil war broke out between farms and I had to defend my property. It cost me my life, leaving Roxy destitute. My friend and her sister took the farm, leaving Roxy victim to wartime abuse, violence and pack rape and before she died, she swore vengeance. Clarification here, I left that lifetime in love. Roxy left in hatred of her nemesis. This emotional twist meant we could not meet in our future life. Roxy judged again generating new fire to flame and now the fun really starts.

Rage is just a four-letter word it means nothing. Roxy created an emotion from her feelings called rage. This emotion was to define her through several of her next life times. We shared this life but on opposite sides of the fence. Roxy's rage made her a male soldier with a vengeful mission to destroy and harm every enemy in her path. When she died, she judged the male soldiers again thus becoming one.

Unfortunately, I happened to be one of those enemy soldiers. The irony was she was trying to kill my friend again and avenge her past. He was in both her past lives as her brother and the friend who evicted her, now he was my friend again and I stood in her aim of fire so she killed both of us. I can see a lot of women here saying, 'you go girl.'

He smiled as he continued. "This woman shows no mercy but the more she strived to exact her revenge the tougher her body armour became; same with mine; now it was my turn. Sounds a bit like my first marriage;" he laughed again, "nah; but yes, some relationships share this in one life time. Roxy and I had several lifetimes to carry it out.

We carried out this tit for tat through several more lifetimes, but what was interesting to note was that my beautiful Roxy had difficulties with weight all her life this lifetime. She was unlike her mother who could eat anything she liked and maintain a lovely svelte physique. Roxy struggled every day since her puberty.

Although she got as well as she gave, her battles were where she was becoming physically stronger and tougher as a human. This is also indicative of her present life.

She had a bad heart and she kept getting backup and fighting.

Now it was my turn. This is where I retaliated and I'm not nice either." He paused, "you say don't get in the way of a mother and her cubs well don't get in the way of some lions either.

I journeyed through crusades, the 100years war, but I also became a Templar knight and met a fiery death. The fracas here is I cannot find

Roxy in our burnings but she was there in an unobvious manner and in her next life, my friend, the same guy again, I seemed to have seen more of him than her." He was quiet for a minute as someone in the audience spoke. "Not in the slightest," he responded to the funny innuendo. "My friend" he cleared his throat "and I were part of a group who were responsible for the burning of the witch heretics of which Roxy was accused. She threw a rock at him and he arrested her along with her mother. I'm the one who ran her through before the fire enflamed her body; nice hey? Every man's dream." He paused again.

"I'm not making any of this up and it was all perfectly legal," he emphasises. "Roxy apparently asked for this to take place to wipe her past lives and clean her slate, so she could start again and I agreed.

Now there is an alteration in our path and Roxy makes another discerned decision to wipe her slate clean. In our next life we marry and we live very happily and I love her unconditionally. She is one third of my life younger than me. We have a child, and she and the child catch the plague and die an early death.

What this strategy does is it clears all past life retributions and heals all the pains. She sacrificed a life of more anguish for one of love but to achieve that she had to leave before she reached 30.

Under normal circumstances you would think we were all finished and healed. No, I hadn't finished my rampage. I was so distraught at her loss I blamed everyone and everything. I didn't want anything around me that reminded me of her so I sold up all things and left and went abroad, trying to forget her. I hated the pain; I hated god; I hated anything that reminded me of our love.

I then lived a life as an Englishman in India who was atrocious to the natives, and behaved badly, until a guru started teaching me higher secrets and that is how I came to be here studying many different philosophies, and looking for proof of everything in this one.

This life time was a journey like many of my others studying, growing, and recreating old mistakes. I married, had a son, divorced, married again divorced, then opened my own hypnotherapy studio and began researching past life regressions and life between life and opening my mind to higher levels of consciousness. I studied it, I learnt it. Roxy knew it; it came so naturally to her.

Roxy after a traumatic life finally decided to open a café in our local town and that's how we met; neither wanting to get married again, neither knowing our path, but our path bought us together.

One day I accidently crashed into Roxy on a footpath and I saw our wedding 1900 years before. I had no idea who she was or where she came from. She told me the same thing however, she had a vision of me killing her with the lance.

As the new local who opened a café on the water front which was organic so yeah this was for me. I enter the café, saw her and the manager informed me she owned the café and studied the sort of stuff I did; past life regression. That information blew me away. When I imagined my future soul mate one of the most important values, I wanted more than anything else was to be able to communicate to her without explanation.

I had been married twice; no more; I was done.

But she… oh she got to me." He smiled as he shook his head. "She talked my language, she understood me, and no one had ever done that to me. We started collaborating on one of my books I found her information more than invaluable.

In the mean time she is seeing my associate hypnotherapist for past life regression. What she discovers is our last existence together and how I reacted badly. So, she takes it upon herself not to inform me because we were so close to achieving our reconnection and she really wanted to reconnect for the next life without any repercussions.

Roxy had a heart condition, and she thought that if we connected in this life again, I would act badly again and she'd lose me again, and we'd have to start all over again.

However, my dad used to say -whoever thinks God doesn't have a sense of humour has never told him his future plans. And as much as I hate to admit it, he's right. Fate took a stand and Roxy had a heart turn and I for a while panicked. So, my associate sought permission to show me her file. I read it and all the information I told you was basically in her file conjoined with mine.

I married the love of my all my lives and I will say that losing her again tore my soul apart. We however knew her time was sensitive so we made every moment count. Roxy toured with me and we had a ball." Some applause echoed through the room. "Oh, I have some old fans, thank you. A photo of Roxy shines on the screens behind him with the date of her life span, and applause rings out again.

He turns around to look upon it and wells up inside.

"Yep that's my girl." He lets the applause die down.

"I was at the end of my tether screaming at her to give me a reason why I should stay because again everything around me reminded me of her. I didn't want the pain. I had lost her all over again. I told her I'd be different this time, but I wasn't. This tearing of my soul was devouring me. Roxy would say I have a brilliant imagination, well she was right.

When I landed on my back, the realisation that I had created victim mode by choice, due to past life perceptions; it was instantly replaced by this new overwhelming feeling of joy. And this amazing feeling was my freedom, speaking again It was my huge ahaa moment. I felt Roxy was with me. And because of my love that I created for us, for her, she will always be with me. Why, because I created it that way.

She knows what is in my heart and she gives it to me through our united love. That's what I created and that is what I want to give to you. The right to choose the path you want to take regardless of how crazy it appears to others.

This amazing gift of your emotional creativeness is yours to keep and it is your connection to your ultimate love. If you are married and you feel you are with your soul mate then treat them with the love they deserve; for when you do the gifts from that love is unconditionally universal and limitless."

He stands from his stool and walks to the front of the stage, "Limitless is an amazing word but until you start using it you will never understand the meaning of it. You don't have to worry about anything for with your creativeness you will always be provided for with all the things you want and need and more.

Quick story there is a guy in our town honestly you could file your toenails with him he is so grouchy and rough.

His beautiful wife came to one of my seminars and started working on him; I nearly died when I saw them walking hand in hand. No one is untouchable by this stuff. When you want it, use it and don't stop ever.

If you don't feel you are with your soul mate, do the same thing. The obstacle is with you. This person is informing you of the element that is victimising you. For it is in the learning to love you that you will find your true love. You both may have to fix up a couple of blockages that are preventing you from going forward. Love anyway and pretend they are your soul mates; the practice will do you good. You are not betraying them it has all been prearranged and allowed.

This is for you; what's that song 'if you can't be with the one you love; love the one you're with,' but be honest.

Between Roxy and me, we had roughly 10 lives to bring us together. Not all paths lead back to love. If you have blockages that are preventing you from reaching your soul mate, heal them now knowing that in doing so you are creating a future of ultimate happiness.

See one of our biggest problems is the ignorance that we don't keep walking through lives; that reincarnation does not exist. The second biggest challenge is we don't believe we create the lives we have to experience. Once we get past that blockage, we can start preparing longer term more fabulous outcomes.

If you notice men were only the ones who crucified; women altered their gender when fiery fierce energy was required. Even though this world is dictated to by a strong male destructive energy, women weaker recipient energy, know that both altered genders to use the same tools to serve that same purpose for them.

That's why it is important to recognise that although you are men and women in this life time you may not have always been. So, blaming men only is not the answer. Recognising that the destructive emotion which you created to experience these entire disastrous situations was actually created by both genders at different times, therefore we are all responsible for the situation of the world today.

Some people use food to display their body of history, material possessions are another way of crushing your soul in to oblivion. The more you desire anything material, homes, money, power, possessions, fortresses, the more you are explaining to yourself you are out of control. You will then keep struggling to maintain it and possessing it wanting more. Wanting more what?

You will cover it up with distractions, sports, work, addictions, and all the unnecessary things, where you don't have to think about it. Running, hiding and cocooning yourself against it for the pain is too unbearable and it is the heart rendering to the worst degree you can imagine; but to admit that you know the way to stop it, but it is too soppy so go away and leave me alone, is sheer suicide.

What I found out while lying flat on my back has doubled my love so Roxy and I could be one in that love. Now, according to me my lovely Roxy can use the wind to comb her fingers through my hair. I can smell her in the blossoms, the beach and my chai coffee every morning. She is not lost. She is with me every single moment of the day and I am alone, but because I presumed the situation was different, I pushed it all away. I separated, she didn't.

Then weird things started happening." He waited for a response, "You're saying that stuff wasn't weird enough now there's more? Oh yeah!" he tantalisingly continues. "Now that you are connected to this universal force you have opened the door to universal weird with a capital "W" giggling could be heard all around the audience.

"Jason the chef of Roxy's café started making unusual cakes and food and they were really nice and unfamiliar. He asked if I believed that Roxy was still around, I had to agree with him.

He said he was never really been this creative before.

Your life alters when you have that love You lose the imprisonment of the material need to have material things because you receive better things.

Due to tragic circumstances, I lost my last promoter and needed a new one;" Raising his hands up and physically thanking his new team he says in a loud accolade "hey what do you think good job?" The audience applauded; he quietened down "I'll say yeah;

I never knew this group existed and they came to me and they are excellent. Thanks guy's great job.

Was our amazing attitude of love responsible?

I like to think so but because of my new attitude I walk with every day, I know so.

So, let's get you to the place where you can acquire all you need. Now I'll be honest I already have my soul mate, but as my Roxy said, if you need me as the stepping stone to help you achieve that new level of unconditional love I have tapes, books and I now have a blog with E books as well. Use them, dream, create, and most of all love yourself.

The Prophet

If you need Jesus or Gandhi, or Buddha use them to raise your level of love, refrain from judging because what you judge you will become. That's what kept happening to Roxy and me. That's what kept pulling us apart; judgement or criticism of a circumstance which we then became. We then had to undo, and then had to balance. You can take that path to test your soulmates resilience, but believe me, it's a hell of a lot nicer holding them in your arms forever." He smiled and winked at the audience. He took a pause.

"The reason Roxy and I are pleading to the feminine gender is as Roxy puts it, the boys like their rough and tumble; women want to be loved. Men think the love thing a bit weak and sissy; football is much more fun; "

He waits for the audience to re- settle.

"Oh yeah we love our rough and tumble and the rougher the better, but that won't bring us all the lifestyle we can have without asking for or being enslaved. So, what we are saying is; women go for it. Go for the unconditional soul mate love that you deserve. When we men can no longer have the rough and tumble without you, many of us will choose you over it.

Once you join the women you automatically get the rough and tumble; they just don't want to be the ball. And when the men are on the receiving end of that rough and tumble, they aren't too impressed either so this act may not be as difficult as it looks.

As the finale starts up on the big screen another huge photo of Roxy and Jai together is displayed. It is the dedication in his book. "Why did Roxy maintain her illness? It was a heart defect. She had it from birth.

When I cast her aside in our last existence it broke her heart. She bought it with her to teach me not to do it again. She died early to regain her clean slate again, and she left me behind because I still had issues to resolve and a huge job to do on behalf of both of us.

Anger, rage, loss did not exist in my life before Roxy died. I created it after she died, to try control something I thought I couldn't control. I felt powerless at her loss, so I became a victim to my powerlessness However within a very short time that powerlessness had total control of me. Roxy leaving had to be reconciled within me. Our love did that for me so I could be one again. I have reconciled my soul to that love and truthfully, I have to be one of the few people who now count down to the days until he dies lovingly.

When Roxy was alive, I feared the day she died, but she said count the days till we are together again. Each day is one day closer. She said, finish what you have to do, then come home to me, I'll be waiting. That was so cool; no one ever said that to me before. Hurry home.

My best friend says I'm a sick puppy," everyone laughs, so does he; "He may be right, but because I am connected to my imaginings of her as that unified love and our love each day is extremely happy and I don't fear death, so I live every day to the fullest knowing every step is a memory to take with me.

Unlike Roxy who knew her time was short; I don't know when mine is due. I live to live and I will die happy knowing that by letting go of my victimised creativeness and reacting to all around me and that we arranged all of this as information telling us what to release, so we can all acquire ultimate happiness, make each day easier to understand. Meaning you get better at it the more you practice it.

Learning to accept death as a huge part of life is releasing one of our biggest fears. When we are separated from our soul mate, or anyone we love unconditionally, children, family, loved ones, I reckon it echoes our first death, our first rendering of our broken heart and now our fear of death due to that intense pain, we react badly to, is creating this huge fear that truly shouldn't exist. We're only changing garments; guy to girl, coloured to white, slave to wealthy aristocrat. We alter our perception on earth, now we have to live it. So, a hibernation period is needed to make the alterations. That's how I see it. You couldn't do the alterations on earth, now that would be really freaky." He laughs with the reaction of the audience.

"Death has us still afraid of it and imprisoned in that fear; however, when you know you are returning to that most amazing of loves and lovers that is the ultimate freedom. That is a joy you want to return to and experience again. Make that one of your most inspiring goals.

When you realise that, you release all the religious doctrinated fear of the unknown. You are returning to the most magnificent love of all time. There is no hell, there is no purgatory; there is no sin; meaning, there is nothing to fear, only unbelievable happiness. If you want it, go get it, if you don't, have fun anyway you'll get it in the end. The trick is you have to believe you already have it. And life happily ever after is one of them.

There's a colloquialism Roxy would use -it will all be right in the end, and if it isn't; then it isn't the end.-

With that I'll say good night folks, hope you enjoyed our night; I certainly enjoyed sharing my love with you. Thank you to my crew you have been extraordinary. You have been a fabulous audience see you again soon. Drive home safely and have a fabulous life, brilliant death and an extraordinary future life, love all of you.

He raises his hands up to wave good bye

"My name is Jai Tagore and from my beautiful wife Roxy Tagore, who this seminar is dedicated to, and myself, I wish to thank you for letting me share her amazing love and I wish you all a Goodnight."

As he leaves the stage the music starts the lights come back on and the doors open for the audience to leave.

Not perfect; areas need tweaking but all in all he got his message across. He had to have a conference with his crew, then he went back to his unit to prepare for his long journey. He discussed areas he wanted to adjust and they adapted accordingly.

He received feedback from the audience through his team and it was considered successful. Book sales were phenomenal, and they need to order more for the tour. It appeared to be more successful than he first anticipated. He decided to go home and try to sleep. He has a long haul ahead of him.

The audio truck left for the night haul to the next town. The arena will be all set up long before Jai gets there. This next show is already sold out so it was proving his theory that the path is created before you even walk it. He was enjoying his new found success. It was an entirely new scale of promotion. He missed his beautiful offsider. He missed her jokes and fun. But this was his first without her, maybe he'll get better. He was responsible for a crew of workers and so far, the sales of tickets for the shows, books and other spoils were creating more than enough for the tour. He smiled, "Roxy you'd be proud love."

He loved sharing his love with people. She felt more alive when he was talking about her. He was thinking he might add some of her quirkier anecdotes and stories if he has time. The barking owl, the ice cream over and above, the shop lifter and the black onyx, they all had him mesmerised.

Jai packed his car for his long six-week tour. His new promoters preferred him in classy light weight suits with various coloured shirts to highlight his dark suit. His dark curly hair was trimmed and neatened but allowed to remain long. His new image was no longer one of casual performer it now was one of class and distinction and professionalism with that touch of sexy salaciousness. Now when he walked on stage, he was welcomed with open arms from his adoring audience, a more mature audience and some old friends

CHAPTER 14

JAI'S FINAL TOUR.

Jai tweaked his tour and became hugely successful and was accepted nationwide. Now there were other towns and other speakers who wanted to join his crew so for the next ten years Jai's life was filled with writing, speaking, and performing. These tours were in auditoriums, tours to exotic areas, cruises, and universities.

He would average five to six solo tours per year and several travel platforms with other speakers in between tours. His life was his work and his work was his life. He didn't retire as much as life retired him.

When he was on his break he would always return to his beach where he found solace with his loving Roxy. They would talk and reminisce for hours. The warmth of the sun the softness of a breeze, the squawking of a gulls, all meant Roxy was with him all the time, but he felt her more at his beach than anywhere else.

He was aging now and his tours were becoming less. He was still in demand and his books were almost always a huge success as soon as they hit the shelves. They now always spoke about the perfection of all things and the unconditional love of all beings and all things in life. He was walking proof of his ideologies. He received everything he ever needed and more and he didn't have to physically ask for it.

He laughed as this was the way his life was truly. He always received it and more, before he even thought of it because the path was created long before he walked it.

He explained it this way; the birth of a child is destined long before the mother is pregnant. The pregnancy is predetermined at least one hundred years before. That's why there is no such thing as an accident. The child, the mother and the father's paths are all destined to collide long before they meet. It may be a one-night stand, but every component of that triste had been synchronistically orchestrated years in advance.

An abortion has been orchestrated years before it takes place. The child and the mother need this action to play out so the child can return within a short period for a higher mission with the same DNA. The interesting path to be observed is of those who sit in judgement due to their lack of true knowledge, for this too is their deemed path.

They will judge, criticize and condemn this act as murder. Their judgement and the extent to which they publicize it is preparing them to follow in the same path. If you too wish to follow like a sheep then be our guest, but you do not have to follow that path, this is where you have freedom of choice. Wouldn't it be so much nicer if you prepared a path of absolute bliss? So why create the reactionary other?

How do you handle it? You realise that the path of the abortion has been preordained for a higher purpose by the mother and the child. The child may need the information of the mother so he/she can return to the mother as a grandchild and this is the only way it can return without acquiring the entire mother's past life DNA.

Another redeeming act is when a child who would have displayed destructive behaviour as a parent in a past life, asks his parent in this life to demonstrate the same behaviour, so he will not do it to his children in his adult life. Without their malevolence he would never have achieved the breaking open of his soul to be the adoring parent that they are. By loving his children, he retrieves his soul from his hatred and theirs.

Over the next few years, the actions of the world depicted his seminars and his books. It created live actions that could be acted upon on a daily basis. His principles remained the same but now he was able to personify them in daily life, this made him more popular than ever.

This path had been provided for him through his undying love. This created love gave him the potential to follow something that made him completely happy instead of worrying and fretting about the money and material means to survive.

Fear or love, both paths are open to you at all times, but one looks difficult because you need to pay bills and eat food and survive according to the material concept of living. Once you swap the need to live principle with the "learn to love and allow" principle, huge changes take place in your life.

That second path to unlimited happiness is open to you, and that path provides unlimited income, proficient business opportunities, wonderful reliable friends, and unlimited doors open that you never imagined. This path provides the over and above bucket list. In other words, you receive more than you ever dreamed of.

Jai's passion for life exuded from his very being at every seminar and platform, and it was contagious. Audiences left with enthusiasm and motivation to alter their way of thinking and desiring more of the best for themselves; but more than anything else they wanted that love of their true soul mate forever and were prepared to make changes to achieve it. They left wanting more, they were already prepared to attend his next seminar or read his next book; they could not get enough.

Jai remained healthy for many of his years of writing and working. In his late eighties he started slowing down. His son arranged for a personal nurse to help with the extra activities he couldn't handle.

Later he arranged for him to be moved to a more convenient place but it had to be within distance of the beach. As he reached ninety, he retired. Each day he would be taken out in his wheel chair to his favourite spot on his beach which now donned a fancy park for visitors with wheel chair access. His loving nurse would bring him down every day and he would talk to his loving Roxy. "Not long now lovely" and he would smile in happiness. The nurses thought him cute how he talks to his departed wife and how he loved her so much.

Sometimes Jesse would come down to join him and bring him a chai. They shared many memories and times gone by. Gary's son was running the studio now so that was the third-generation hypnotherapist. Gary too was a grandfather, so Jai's family had expanded in to the fourth generation; yes, he had left quite a legacy. This was his unfinished work. Val too had grandchildren and she would keep in contact from time to time. This relationship developed due to Jai's book of their marriage and love. She saw her mother in a new light and liked it.

Jason too handed his restaurant over to his celebrated chef son and it still belonged in the bay. Roxy's love had expanded throughout the bay and touched everyone in one way or another, but nobody knew.

Jai was pleased he didn't leave the bay in his time of relentless pain. He's glad he went to the beach that day. He would never have seen the abundance provided for all the bay had he left.

The pain he caused his Roxy in the previous life by destroying her attempts to help him heal prevented her from helping the area the plague perpetrated to heal. Now he understood.

PART 2

THE DRUIDESS

CHAPTER 15

HIRING JASON

Roxy had inherited some money and she decided to become productive with it. Her daughter and family saw her as weird and eccentric. In their world, she was someone who needed caring after.

Roxy had a talent where she would read tarot cards and was able to reveal past connections to their present life and from that, challenge them to a better future by understanding that what was within them was causing all their fluctuations in this life. It was a profitable business but her family connections found it absurd because none of them understood how she became so talented in her field of interpretation.

She had been looking for a new home and saw a business advertised at an extremely low price near a bayside kiosk in the bay area; so, she decided to take a look. It needed a serious amount of work but her budget allowed for it. It truly was love at first sight. As she walked away a couple waved, "looking at buying?" She smiled and nodded. "That'd be great. We miss the old place" That was the deciding factor. The customers were nice and friendly. "Yes," and she now already had two patrons.

The kiosk over looked the water and she decided to take advantage of that. She went into the real estate agency and they showed her the inside of the property. The kitchen needed upgrading. There was a small café inside and wear and tear but nothing she couldn't handle. She paid for it outright; now she owned a café kiosk. She now needed a plan of action. This was extremely impulsive and Roxy loved the exhilaration and felt alive.

What's that colloquialism she thought? "It'll be right in the end; and if it isn't; then it isn't the end" She now needed a good manager, some staff, a carpenter, someone who can put in a coffee machine, grinders, kitchen, cake cabinet, new tables, a few chairs. The carpark needed grading, and the view needed perking up. Oh yeah, she also needed a place to live; that would be nice.

Roxy didn't expect to make such a sudden decision so now she also had to sell the family home. This may not go down as easily as originally thought with the family, but she was moving on and living her own life now. They all wanted her nearer to them in some aged care facility; but this was the furtherest thing on Roxy's mind. Roxy had a bad heart and there always was an issue with her dying early but she wasn't going to die soon. Roxy genuinely wanted to live first.

Her house sold quickly and she moved into a quaint one bedroom, Wedgewood blue and white cottage. It was ideally situated near the café and close to town.

Her move went easily and to Roxy this was a good omen and meant smooth sailing so this added to the excitement to start the kiosk. Now she was centralised and could work more easily. Contractor quotes, and staff, and plans all had to be organised. She spoke to the realtors about good workmen and the local shopping area for new staff.

Within a week huge renovation began; stripping and repairing the area. Contractors for a newly designed kitchen, expresso machine, and catering cabinet combination of hot and cold that went in a surround in front of the kitchen which was nicely opened enough for the customers to view.

The kiosk would open to customers passing through or staying the day at the bay for fishing or body board riding. In the warmer months the kiosk was extremely active but in the cooler months the café would supply the needs of most of the clients. Roxy saw all this happening. This was her new life and it was exciting. She could cook mainstream food but her dream speciality was raw organic and natural food all made with natural ingredients.

Word was spreading around the bay that a new café was opening and they were looking for new staff. Jason worked in a local café. While going home one night, he became the victim of a gay bashing by the local thugs.

Within a week he went to apply for a position in the new opening café on the bayside. He put some makeup on his face to cover the bruises and tried to cover up all other forms of indignation that might impair his opportunity of success. His confidence was low.

He was the last of three contenders who appeared extremely confident. He'd never seen them before but they seemed very chummy. He waited his turn; held his head up high and walked in with a smile and laid all his credentials on the desk for Roxy to read.

Roxy lowered her head as she read his material and smiled to herself. She asked her usual questions, and then she brazenly said, "I hope he won."

"Pardon me" responded Jason feeling a little unprepared. Roxy stood up; walked around toward him; gave him a wet cloth to wipe off his make-up and repeated her statement. "I hope he won;" she paused for moment then continued as she returned to her seat with a smile. "He was supposed to win, "she continued.

"They," he butted in;

She nodded, smiled and continued. "You see if you had won, I would not have known who to hire."

His head rose as he looked at her totally baffled. "I asked for an omen for the greatest manager who would be the best for the bay in this café. I think yours is pretty obvious, don't you?" she smiled.

She tossed her hand up and persisted "Oh you'll get used to it; unconventional, weird, eerie yes I'm all of those but you were the only one who held his head up high, and you had more to hide."

"You mean I've got the job" stammered a bumbling Jason.

"If you want it," answered Roxy. She introduced herself and shook his hand.

"You are remarkable but you don't know it yet," she emphasised. "Forgive me. I presume you have a male partner, and that is why you were punished. You allowed them to win, of course, because they are following in your footsteps. That's why you are here. You and your partner are soul mates. The love you both cherish is the love they are searching for.

Weird I know, but with every judgement of you and all those like you, your persecutors are depicting is their future path. You and your partner are their future. You are here this way purposely informing everyone that this type of love can conquer all unbeatable odds. All your judges are following in your footsteps because they want what you have.

You and your partner have endured all the sadness, pain, loneliness, and emptiness they are suffering now. You've been through it and now you are here; was it worth it?

The only way they'll experience the same amazing love you and your partner are experiencing is to follow in your footsteps. The only way they will obtain it is to judge you, criticise you, and every disparaging judgement they persecute toward you is another notch in their belt to their future path of the unconditional love like yours.

So, if you want to really piss them off, and get even with them; display your love even further. The reason I'm telling you this is because, this is who I am. This is who you will be working for. I already see you as a fabulous leader, so now tell me if you still want the job."

Jason stood up; held out his hand as happiness exploded out of every morsel of his body. "When do I start?"

"Now too soon," mirrored a very joyous Roxy.

As Roxy showed him the new restaurant he would be in charge of and the plans for expansion, he had to query her previous statement. "You mean all the people who condemn us, are following us?"

Roxy interrupted with laughter, "Yes! Makes you laugh at the churches the politicians and the holy do gooders who are literally paving a way in the same direction, doesn't it?'

Roxy was in full bore laughter by now. She then put her hand on her hip and swaddled away "walk this way" she collapsed with laughter. "That's why no saviour was needed, everything is perfect the way it is. I know I'm a kook but I'd rather look at life with love than hate and fear."

"Back to work," Roxy asked if he needed alterations and how would he like to handle all of it to achieve maximum turnover. Roxy wanted to create a veranda with nice chairs and tables surrounding the café, and it would need to have protection from the sun and wind.

"Jonah" was his response. "He creates the most amazing furniture." He paused a moment, "sorry, he's my partner." Before they knew it, they arranged to go see Jonah's work and had worked out how they would place each piece to create an ambiance in this new look café. They both bounced ideas of each other and this relationship was proving to be extremely proficient.

MEETING JONAH

Jason arranged for Jonah to show his new boss his work. Jonah worked privately designing and manufacturing timber work mostly but he was an engineer and was able to design huge structures as well. He was a stay at home dad and he and Jason had a seven-year son. The son would hang around the yard and the shed, when he wasn't sailboarding with Jonah, while he created. Jonah was tall, dark and solidly built due to his hard-toiled labour.

Roxy walked into an immaculately set up business displaying various ornamental designed seats, chairs and tables. His splendid array made it difficult to make a discerned decision. Both she and Jason then asked for Jonah's input. Both Jason and Jonah knew the area much better than Roxy so this input would be vital to the ongoing success of the alfresco effect Roxy wished to introduce to the area.

Jonah decided he would design a special type of swivel seat that could not move at the same time rotate for customer comfort. He could attach the table to the deck so they wouldn't move on breezy days. He would use a local timber and local stone for the table tops.

When Roxy saw the final design, she agreed swiftly and asked if he would consider doing all her work including the deck.

This was the beginning of a long and loving relationship.

When Jonah started creating the covered veranda, he proposed another concept that he had been thinking about for the aged people around the area. They have been neglected and they love their chess and board games. He could build stone chess tables and they could come and play chess by the bay. All he had to do would be to expand the veranda at one end and open it up.

Roxy was stoked at the idea. This act of unbelievable love would open so many doors for so many people especially if they weren't asking for anything in return. Wow this place will exceed expectations. "*It is in the giving that you receive.*" Roxy asked for the best this town could offer and she received people who followed her principles. This was the happiest she had ever been in her life.

Time was passing faster than expected and the grand opening was approaching quickly. The place looked as if it wouldn't be ready in time. Jason had to hire staff who were experienced and capable of using the new equipment. They had to prepare a menu in both fast lane and organic, and a creative assistant chef who could create the new recipes not found anywhere else.

Jason was preparing all the last-minute arrangements and becoming stressed as the time became shorter. Jonah's work was proving to be both successful and creative, but their relationship was feeling the strain.

While Jason was stressfully working on the recipe boards, Jonah waltzed in with his one hand on his hip and the other raised in his drag queen persona, with his pinkie extended and goaded "Hmm what about a zucchini slice with watermelon?" Jason looked up in frowned astonishment 'Wha."

"No, you're right, too moist" he continued as he puckered his lips, "Oh this place is simply too much for my creative juices" he incited as he strutted out to the door.

"And you've got to stop watching kinky boots" responded Jason in disgust. Jonah turned and nipped "maybe you should start." Then he twaddled out with a back kick.

With that Roxy joined Jason at the table "what was that about?"

"Oh, it's just his way of saying ease up," as Jason maintained his working persona. "He's not really like that you know."

"Oh, I know; it was the funniest thing I've seen all week." She laughed. "Maybe you should take his advice."

"What zucchini and water melon?"

Roxy split her sides with laugher. "Nooo; ease up, this place will open whether we have pretty boards or not. It's not a one-day event where we only have one chance. We will be open for some time. What we don't finish at grand opening we can render the day after and after that. It's almost done, the extras are superficial. Do me a favour. That man loves you and he cares for you so much. Why don't you take him home and" then she bent close to his ear and whispered "fuck him into the next century"

"Language" said a stunned Jason.

"I'm not afraid of the f bomb." said Roxy "The word truly doesn't exist. However, people emotionally react to it and personify it giving it life. The English language is the most amazing expressive language to learn. It has adjectives that scintillate the nouns so you can taste them, feel them, touch them; and there is no other word in the English language that can express our most amazing act of unbelievable union. Especially when used sexily and intoxicatingly to allow the true measure of it to express it. It is an act of fabulous fornicational power at its best. I mean what I say. Go and give him a smacker for me" she got up to walk away "A kiss: I meant a kiss," she laughed.

Jason got up to leave and smirked as he began to walk out, "I might give him both" he salaciously replied.

Roxy laughed; she had truly been blessed with amazing loving people, she screeched and stomped her feet with exultation. This was more than a dream; this was her future lives taking shape now. In front of her were happy people who loved and cared for each other sensually, sexually and genuinely. They were showing her the path she wanted to follow so much. This immense happiness was her ultimate desire; to be joined with someone to love in complete unity and undying love.

Roxy finished the boards and closed down the café then locked it safely. She was living her dream. The café passed all inspections health and safety wise; this was really happening and it was looking brilliant. Roxy altered the kiosk's name to "Water café and kiosk."

CHAPTER 16

CLASH WITH DESTINY

Roxy was returning back from the advertisers preparing a huge page announcing the grand opening. She was rushing amid crowds that were all coming the other way. Roxy's handbag started slipping off her shoulder and as she went to grab it, she crashed into a man coming the other way. The impact forced her to the ground, and she slipped into a lane and stayed down on the footpath till she caught her breath.

While there she felt a heart rendering pain as she saw herself being burned to the stake. There were two men in steel armour on horses in front of her as one through a lance straight into her heart to kill her before the flames engulfed her. She felt the lance enter; then she returned to sanity. This entire experience shook her for several minutes. She thought her heart was having a spasm again. Then a hand reached down for her," you okay love" as it raised her to her feet, "do you need an ambulance?"

"No thank you," she responded as she started brushing her clothes off. The strangers walked on their way as Roxy gathered her thoughts and returned to her office. This event had made the days actions very distracting. She was unable to focus and Jason presumed it was exhaustion and wondered if he could help in any way. "No" answered Roxy, "just a bad dream"

"Well we're ready. Now all we need is customers." He smiled as he touched up the last of the serviettes. This was the nicest place he'd ever worked in. He called his staff and informed them of all their positions and purposes for the opening. He told them what to expect.

They were opening on the Sunday. No one in town opened on Sunday so expect a variety of customers. Tables constantly cleaned including outside. The chess gazebo was set up with six chess tables in glazed stone and stone stools with cushions. Enough room for plates and coffee, but this area is not for normal customers, it set up for chess and board players; dominoes, chess, scrabble, and nongaming cards.

As soon as the last-minute preparations were done, Jason sent his staff home, readying them for tomorrow's grand opening. All the fresh stock has been prepared for service, and they expect the kiosk to be mobbed as soon as the doors are open.

Roxy went home and tried to relax but this was her first grand opening of anything and she was nervous, not because of failure but because of success. She knew there was a lot of excitement in the bay about the opening up again, and the new extensions were an added interest. This would be a learning experience for Roxy and she wanted to know what she needed to do to improve it and fulfil as many of the needs of the bay as possible.

It was a long night for Roxy who was still being tormented by the burning at the stake vision, as well as the opening. All was so fine till that episode. Regardless of what she tried to do; the horror of the lancing kept filling her thoughts.

Jason, Jonah and Daniel were having their last family dinner together for a while. At least up until all settles down and Jason can work out the temperament of the café. He will take time off to be with his loving family on special days but until he can sort the best time to do that, they all have to stretch a little.

Jonah and Daniel decided they were going to support Jason and have lunch at the café where daddy worked tomorrow. It was all planned.

Meanwhile in the local auditorium Jai was experiencing his successful seminar and book sales.

WATERFRONT CAFÉ AND KIOSK
GRAND OPENING

Four o clock in the morning and Roxy was up and ready. She had to open up the kitchen to allow more stock to arrive at five before the cafe opened. Jason would meet her and help her put the stock away. They hoped the truck would arrive on time, because more preparation for fresh food needed to be completed before opening.

All audio and technical computers had to be checked. Registers filled; preparation of tables; condiments and cutlery ready; "Let's do this." Six o clock the door opened and customers were waiting for fresh coffee and morning snacks. It was continuous movement all morning. No one stopped. It ran like a well-oiled machine.

At eight in the morning the door to the café was opened. This opened to the fresco and the chess gazebo. There was a line up to the counter for both food and coffee up to four deep at a time. Hot and cold food was being plated continuously to a full coffee house.

Alex came through the kiosk and gloated about the previous evening's success and about ten minutes later into the café walked Jai. He appeared to be a deep conversation with Jason.

Roxy recognised him as the man who bumped into her. He made her feel uncomfortable. He's the man who threw the spear, she's sure of it, but she couldn't worry about that now, there were too many tables to wipe down so she could place new customers. She bought out Jai's chai and food to his table and he thanked her as she swiftly departed.

"Maybe it wasn't him. Maybe it was someone else" thought Roxy. Back to work. There appeared to no stopping in all departments and this grand opening was extremely successful but it was also extremely tiring.

Roxy had to force herself to leave for a break or she simply would not get one and her feet were becoming really sore. She told Jason she would break for 20 minutes and then he could go. When she sat her entire body slumped into the seat. "It won't always be like this" she mumbled to herself, "just keep going you'll make it."

Next minute Jason came out. "It's right, I'm taking a break there's a lull in the traffic; Matts holding the fort" He sat down and "phew!" he gasped and laughed at the success he was absorbing. His lunch was in the fridge so he served some up for him and Roxy as she wasn't eating "here keep up your strength, I need you out there." He gave her a tasty cashews and vegetable in rice as he knew she was vegan. "You made this?" she queried.

"Yeah it's an old recipe that's healthy," answered Jason with a mouthful of food.

"Can we use it?" asked Roxy as she enjoyed every morsel.

"Already taken care of" responded Jason with a smile on his face at the pleasure that Roxy liked his creation.

Roxy made a quick rest spot check on all the facilities with a quick tidy, then back to work. It had quietened down and there were only stragglers entering now. Some of the staffs were allowed to go home and return on their regular shift. It was a very successful day, and the last hour dragged a bit but when finishing time arrived some very exhausted staffs were happy to close all the doors, have a drink and go home. Lights off, money placed in the safe for banking in the morning, last of coffee cups placed in washing machine for a quick wash and go home.

Roxy relaxed into a hot soaking bath, to take the strain of the days exercise away. With the restless night and the busy day her poor little body was feeling the stress. She added Epsom, rose and lavender salts, to a full tub of hot water and simply let the days jaunts melt into the water.

She seemed to be in there for ages. The water was cooling down. She raised her tired body out of the tub and wrapped it in a towel blanket and made her way to the bedroom where she fell on the bed and went into a deep exhaustive sleep.

Morning came too soon; up at four to meet the food truck as there was no food left in the café from yesterday and it was essential for the days sales. Jason met her at the back door and they both waited for the truck and the fresh supplies. They prepared the kiosk quickly and opened it for passing through traffic, then opened at 8 again for café customers.

The kiosk was utilising heavy traffic on the way to work and had a consistent flow. Then the café opened and the traffic slowed as people were at work and the café provided for the few who would become the regulars; the regular cash flow. A lot of these customers were clients of Jason's in his previous establishment of work. They followed him for he had a good repour with many of them and knew them by name and order.

Jai was one of the customers who followed Jason and became a regular morning chai drinker. After he left Roxy asked about him.

"He's the local hypnotherapist. He and Jesse they run a studio in town. He's like you. He delves in past life stuff and helps people overcome different things. I could introduce you if you like."

"No. What about Jesse, does he do the same thing?"

"Yeah they are exactly the same except Jai write books and Jesse does the tapes and meditation." Jason answered as he kept working on his coffee machine preparing different varieties of coffee for customers.

"Does Jesse ever come in?"

"Can't say I've ever seen him, but that doesn't mean he doesn't come into the kiosk."

With that Roxy walked away and delivered the ordered coffees and cakes to the waiting tables.

Roxy's business was expressing immense happiness throughout the bay. Jonah offered another proposal that would open up another opportunity for wheelchair bearers.

While dining with Daniel, he carried a young lad to the pier so he could fish. His wheel chair could not cross the sand for him to fish so Jonah carried him and returned for him an hour later. This gave him another brilliant idea. It would need council approval and council planning but he could create an extension from the café to the pier for disabled wheelchair customers. He made the suggestion to Jason and he suggested he converse with Roxy and go from there.

It would be a big job and he would need help with Daniel, Jason said "no problems we'll cross that bridge if it happens"

"If? If it happens?" Jonah chided

"When; I meant, when it happens" rebutted Jason.

This lack of confidence was the exact fireball needed to trigger Jonah and insure it did happen. He charged in to Roxy and passionately proposed his new idea. Roxy loved it. She needed a quote and as he said, he would do all the paperwork and he could add it to the veranda and extend from there.

He accentuated, he would draw up plans and show them to both the council and her for approval.

Jonah went home excited about his new idea. He had a hard haul ahead of him. First, he started drawing different designs that would work with the café, the veranda, the carpark. Then there was another path. He could create a ramp to the chess gazebo then a ramp from the gazebo to the pier. It would be smoother and more accessible for all concerned. The ramp would be low scale and the wheelchair entrance would be accessible in both directions. He created a building plan that should be acceptable by the council and Roxy alike.

He called it 'wheel chair accessibility to pier plan'. He also improved the pier so fishermen could lean on a protective guard rail to prevent falling accidents. He orchestrated a quote for Roxy if council approved. He took it in to the council with all proposals necessary. He had to wait for the next council meeting and he had to wait for public approval. He received an overwhelming vote of approval, and the council would subsidise with 50%.

Once approved he needed a start work date from Roxy. She was ecstatic. Within weeks he put up his building preventions signs and called in an earthmover to flatten the sand. He was able to do this and stay home and take care of Daniel, for the workers had the plans and were able to carry out this work without him.

Now Jason had to stick to his end of the bargain. He now had to worry about how Daniel would be taken care of while Jonah worked for three months. Jason arranged for a baby sitter on a temporary basis to care for his son while he worked and he re-arranged his schedule until Jonah had finished his ramps. When all the work was done and Jonah was finished, Roxy arranged a grand opening for this new wheelchair pier accessibility ramp. A ribbon was cut and several wheel chairs pressed on to the pier to fish.

This was another exciting day for the bay for many who again had been forgotten. Young and old now accessed the café for the chess and the fishing and again Roxy realised a small dream. Jesse was one of the new clients who came in to check out the café for coffee. The story of Magnificent Obsession was true. You fulfil other's dreams; yours too will be obtained.

Jason introduced Jesse and Roxy and she asked for his help. There were conditions to his assistance. One; his partner wasn't to know and she could only get away on Mondays. Jesse had a brilliant idea. There is another studio available and he can hire it on Mondays and no one need know but him and her. Roxy agreed.

CHAPTER 17

ROXY'S TREATMENT

When Roxy went for her first treatment, she had to explain to Jesse why she wanted this experience. She tried to inform Jesse of her vision that caused her distress due to the lance. She saw this a fellow as her enemy. Jesse didn't tell her about Jai's experience how he knew this fellow was Jai and how he saw the soul vow. He was hoping that the regressions would give her the information she needed to find the truth.

In Gary's studio there was a warm room with a comfortable bed and a sound audio system that Jesse designed to get the best results for past life regressions. Each session can take up to three hours so complete silence and comfort is dire.

Jesse started getting Roxy to release all her fears and totally relax. He did this up to three times ensuring her safety comfort and deep sleep was created.

Her first life was light and recent, early century. She was alone and studied as an apprentice naturopath whom she loved. She married and her life was quiet and loving. So, Jesse transgressed her further.

During her next regression, she was in spirit mode. She was being crushed and tormented. She was being abandoned, and thrown away. Roxy travelled through a vortex and saw her body lying with hundreds of others on the back of a wagon being thrown into a fire and discarded.

Jesse asked her to travel back to a more memorable time; she was a young teen. She had been given to an older man about twenty-seven, she was married to him. She was running in a grain field and he was chasing her, she was laughing and happy. She turned and faced him and he place her faced in his hands.

He loved her, he adored her; it was Jai, but it wasn't Jai. She could see into his soul through his eyes. They were the same eyes and he was overjoyed with her. Roxy advanced forward and the plague engulfed the nation. She and her child became victims; they died.

He couldn't handle the pain. She tried to help him by showing him that their love was eternal and if he held on to it, she could save him; but he rejected her.

His agony was too severe; he hated everything that reminded him of them, so he left and forgot them. All his rejection divided their love and tore it apart and separated them, and that was their last meeting.

Jesse woke Roxy up slowly telling her she will remember all that took place and until the next appointment more memories of this revelation will appear and she is to write them down for her own records and bring them back with her. This will make the next regression more easily accessible.

Roxy woke easily and was comfortable with what she saw. This was not the vision she saw about a soldier killing her. This time Jai loved her so much; then he rejected her in death. What she never knew before was that when a person has died if the human rejects them, they still feel the rejection as spirit and that reaction by the human will determine the human's future life as if they did it to another human. So even though you are on different planes the rejection from the human format is still recorded within the DNA or their soul and they return to the rejection without you.

This was further evidence for Roxy in the division of the soul from self. She didn't divide their love, he did. His pain divided them. It's not the people, it's the emotion, that determines the future path. They create the painful emotion and that determines their future path. She booked another appointment for the next fortnight and returned home feeling successful.

18

CHAPTER

ANNIVERSARY PARTY

The café was running like clockwork and Jason had acquired outside functions as well. It was becoming the talk of the town, as the place to go. Jason and Jonah had their family time back and Roxy also had personal time.

Jason wanted to hire out the café one night for his and Jonah's wedding anniversary. They allowed several customers to come to join them. This was an exciting time for both of them. Jonah's contribution to the cafés facilities with his carpentry skills played a big part in not only the café décor which made it unique, but with many of the open-air activities as well. They were much loved by many of the local residents.

Jonah walked into the café and he was furious. He thought that with all his work he had over ridden all the prejudice and bigotry. He thought it was all behind him. Jason tried to calm him down but to no avail. He explained to Roxy that the old famed bigoted idiot pack was threatening to sabotage. He held his finger up to gesture inverted commas, "the faggot's night."

Jonah had calmed down and was seated in the corner alone doing paper work. Roxy walked up and said quietly, "I'll get security if you like."

Jonah shunned that idea, "that's not the point"

"Can I throw a penny in the works?"

She asked as she pulled up a chair. "I've done many studies about this sort of thing and I can tell you that you have it back to front, so do they." She smiled as she continued.

The people who judge become their judgement. Their entire judgement and criticism paved their future paths. This path is displayed both ways. If you look at him, that is who you were. You are his future path. That's why I love you two. You are in front of me and you love each other so much, and that's my future path." She started to well up.

"You are leading all of us. So, when you look at those bigoted asses you have to realise that was the path you took to get here. So now you can stand up in front of them and say" as she started express herself with her hands "You don't like this face; you don't like this hair; you don't like this body; you don't like this ass? Shame, cos this ass is gonna look really good on you." He laughed.

"Your hatred opened the door to your love now. That's why they are following in exactly the same way. They too want what you have and they have to do it the same way you did. So, unless you want to react the same way they are and go back and do it all again until you get it right, let them go and show them the way home to ultimate happiness. They deserve it and so do you." Roxy started to leave "let me know about the security"

About half an hour later Jonah walked into her office and gave Roxy a huge hug, "I'm okay about the security, and I'm following you."

"No" Roxy responded, "I don't want you to be lonely ever. I want to follow you into love, all of it. Just watching you two lets me know that I can have the same thing too. And I so want that, you have no idea" She returned his hug, "but that's the nicest thing anyone has said to me today. Thank you," she kissed him on the cheek as they embraced a little longer, then he left.

The café assistant chef prepared a double layer cake in gold brown and crème, surrounded by curled chocolate and ornamental icing. Around the edge was the words "anniversary decade" He catered a three-course meal of Jason's favourite meals. A section of the floor was left open for dancing and a DJ was hired to play all their old favourite songs.

The night was a huge success with many favourite customers and friends. There was no trouble and the couple displayed monstrous love in front of everyone. Roxy welled up several times at their happiness. This was an excellent night for her seeing her future prospects, even if it wouldn't be this lifetime it would be her next; this was definitely a "Yes" moment.

Jai came into the café on the Monday and asked about the whereabouts of Roxy but it was her day off so now he knew she worked weekends and took all Mondays off. He could work with that. He left inferring his continued return.

19
CHAPTER

DIFFERENCE OF OPINION

Tuesday was quiet for the café. It gave the staff time to clean up properly from a usually busy weekend and Mondays. Windows, floors, extra scrubbing under the tables and the outside shrubs and garden were preened and tidied. The pathways given an extra scrub and any paint chips reported for maintenance.

Jai decided to try to talk to Roxy. He was looking for new input on his new book. All his books were beginning to appear samey so fresh ideas would assist. Jason being his friend would tell him about the conversations they would have and these intrigued Jai because although they were similar to his teachings, she was looking at it from a new refreshing perspective.

Jason also informed Roxy of his conversations with Jai and she agreed to meet. She had nothing to lose. Maybe it would curb her apprehension toward him.

Jai arrived on the Tuesday morning and sat at his usual table in the corner where he had the best view of all that was happening. Roxy bought out his chai and cake and carried out the normal formalities. Jai asked "do you have time to talk? Jason has offered your services for my seminars and we are seriously considering them."

"That's what you want to talk about?" queried Roxy catching him out. He blustered a bit and she said,

"You're not a good liar and that's not a bad thing. Yes, I have time to talk. I'll just get myself a drink and join you if that is ok." Jai nodded feeling embarrassed at his lack of confidence around her.

When she joined him, she stated that she is still working but she has time to sit. She sat so she could see incoming customers who needed attendance.

"I don't really know where to start" commented Jai. He explained that he does past life regressions and life between life existences and from that he is able to inform people that life is a continuum, based on previous judgements. He added that what people see around them is their past and what they see in front of them is their future.

The conversations flowed backwards and forwards as Roxy explained that what we are seeing is people following each other. He hadn't quite thought of it that way but yes that is a possibility. She then pointed out that she would probably be considered contentious, but if he was to take his body history into consideration how would he explain his colouring, his dark eyes, his background, not only his path, but why is he the exact form that he is?

Jai was intrigued; he sat back sipping his chai and let her continue as she waved her hands around as if playing a musical instrument as she spoke.

Then with exhilaration Roxy started; "what if the staircase to happiness started with the white supremists who with all their bigotry, racism, hatred, war and genocide are actually on the lowest rung of the ladder and all the other races are the stepping stones to higher magnificent nothingness and they are all following behind according to prejudice, bigotry, colour, race and creed. What if the path we have to take is exactly the path we are all taking?"

Jai smiled and became sensually excited as she displayed her excited passion for her beliefs.

"In order for us to rise up the ladder we have to both execute and experience the same path as the person in front of us."

"So, we are all finding our path home?" he questioned

"No;" she paused and rearranged her thoughts. "More than that; we already know our way home. It is simply a matter of following a path and according to the level of our supremist accusations and judgements it will depict where you are in the pecking order on the ladder.

We accuse a black man for being black, so our next adventure is the very accusation with which we accosted them. Doesn't that excite you? It means none of us are lost as the religious teachings insist on informing us. We are all simply experiencing the path to the top of the ladder. The perpetrator is at the bottom and the victim is at the top."

He smiled and let her continue as he tried to visualise what she was saying.

"The rich, the mighty, the politicians, the religious autocrats, royalty, governments who are dictating supremists over everyone else are actually through their actions predicting their future path as the lowest on the rung. The very people they are presuming to be lessor than they, are in front of them not behind.

So, let them carryon with their supercilious attitude because next life time they will be the self-same guttersnipe they accuse others of being. Don't you get it? The more you have, the less you are. The more stuff you have the heavier it is for you to rise." She paused for a second, "sorry I'm rambling on," and she sat back.

"Your theory to racism would certainly bite racism in the backside." Jai had to laugh and thought her comments very provocative and although he may not place that in his orations, it certainly made him think on a wider scale.

"Only if you believe racism exists. It only exists if you need it to," she retorted. "If you need it to exist, then that is the path you will travel; oh god I'm off again, sorry." Jai took both her hands "don't ever apologise for what you say, you are one of the most refreshing and interesting people I've ever spoken with; your ideas amazing." He let her hands go and sat back again.

"Please, continue" he stated with a frown on his face.

"Racism doesn't exist until someone is in front of you that you feel intolerant about. Then in your mind you create a feeling of racism. But it is only your perception of the person in front of you it still doesn't exist. You created it, now it will define you as a racist."

"Can I use some of this stuff for my next seminar? Of course, I need to speak to you more an get it right but I would love to hear more if that's okay with you."

"Yes, that'd be fine. Sorry have to go, customer; yes, but we can do this again if you can handle my jabber." She quickly left.

"Wow!" Jai smiled as he sighed. He finished his drink placed it on the counter waved to Roxy and casually left, but he felt more than casual. His body was reacting to the encounter. This woman stirred up emotions he hadn't felt in a long time.

"Maybe Einstein is right; *'The sexiest thing to encounter is an intelligent conversation*,' well he didn't say it quite like that but wow that was certainly a sexy conversation. Her eyes sparked as she spoke; her smile; those hands; those dancing hands;" he breathed out heavily; "Wow" he gasped.

He had to return to the studio as he had clients but it was a different person returning back than the one who left. His spirits had lifted and he was displaying feeling of happiness. Jesse made a comment, but Jai didn't tell him of his meeting just yet; he wanted to keep these feeling to himself.

The café was business as usual; however, Jason put forth a proposal to have a night functions like his anniversary night. Weddings, birthdays, anniversaries, but they had to get a licence. This would make them more than simply a café. Now they were looking at a restaurant approval. These plans required a few alterations. A dance floor needed to be added to the café and proper amenities for a different crowd.

Roxy agreed, now it was the councils turn. It would still be only small functions no more than 100 but the new designs made it possible. A bar and correct storage for alcohol and wines, non-tap, bottles only. This would also open up an area for selling alcohol and cold drinks to the fishermen on the weekends in a restricted area.

Roxy's appointment with Jesse was due and she kept her diary of new developments. She gave her diary to her therapist and they discussed different objectives she wanted to experience. Did she want to return to the same time or go back further to see what initiated this experience? Roxy chose to explore further if possible.

Second session, name, date, and the time were all entered on her chart. Jesse set up the audio ready to record everything that is said. He started the automatic deep sleep hypnotic music and words that infiltrated the theatre she was resting in. He watched her carefully as she was successfully seduced into a deep trance with comfort and assurance of her complete safety at all times.

He took her back through her timeline redressing the episodes that she had already experienced, once there she now started the next part of her journey. Reconnecting her to that life, she was now to go deeper into the trance of karmic resolution that created that path.

Roxy started rocking from side to side as if she was trying to avoid something. Jesse coached her to step out of the picture and see it from above in a third-party perspective. She rose out of her body and saw her body tied to a bushel of brush as she was tied to a picket and being burned to the stake.

"Let's go back further to a happier time;" he waited awhile; "what is your name?" There was a long pause, "Bree; I'm Brianna;" Little by little Bree starts tell her story of a beautiful young girl whose father was behind in his taxes. The Hierarchy had taken everything they owned, including Bree. Her mother took in healing people around the area using herbs and old remedies. Due to religious politics of the old neighbour Bree's mother was accused of heresy. Soldiers came and took her away. Bree tried to fight one of the soldiers. He threw her on the ground. She picked up a rock and pelted it at him. It hit him hard, so he arrested her as well. They were accused of atrocities that didn't exist but they had no defence so they were sentenced to being burned to the stake to cleanse their immortal souls from heresy.

They were dragged out of their prison with a rope around their neck. This was used to choke them before they were burned to death. They were tied to the stake. The shrubs caught fire quickly and they couldn't get to the ropes quickly enough, so a soldier threw his lance straight into her heart. Their eyes connected just before he threw his lance. They were filled with compassion. He couldn't see her suffer. He was simply doing his job, no more. He was the king's soldier.

Roxy died quickly, and when she crossed over, she discovered it was her soul mate again. This death was agreed upon by both of them to cleanse her soul of past offences, so they could be together in their next life. However, his actions would create an obstacle between them, so their time together would be short for he had to lose her unjustly.

Jesse decided to bring her out of this quite dramatic past life experience. He told her she would remember this life more as a movie as oppose to an actual experience. Again, he reminded her that other avenues of this experience would unfold naturally and she was to record them in her dairy.

He explained that she would wake up refreshed, however, Roxy felt exhausted. This was when Roxy explained that she had seen this before.

She told Jesse she was walking past Jai and she bumped him and this memory overwhelmed her. However, he saved her life. He did it to save her the cruel pain of burning to death. Her accusations were false, so that meant she bought this upon herself. This was her path. It also explained why she died in her next life.

"What a mess I've created," she put her face in her hands, "will I ever get it right?" She sat a while with Jesse and he counselled her.

Again, she made another appointment to find out what caused all of this, two weeks hence. "See you then."

Colder months were now ensuing and the waterfront was getting a beating from the winds. Fishing died off except for the really warm days. Chess gazebo was constantly empty, too cold, but the new restaurant was supporting the entire café. Now it was a licenced restaurant at café prices with coffee. This was one of Jason's brilliant ideas and it was their ace in their hole. Without it, winter could have proven to be a tight budget period.

This slow period made it easier to talk with Jai and the conversation spanned many different areas that Roxy was passionate about. Body history was always high on her agenda. She explained how the past history of the human body is deemed in the physical appearances and illnesses experienced today.

As she says the soul is non-gender, non-colour, and non-creed, all these imprisoning limitations become us when we enter our individual dimensions. Obesity, addictions, violence, peace, religious, there are millions; but each and every one of them are paths inadvertently chosen by us to walk; however, our appearance depicts the dimension we will enter. The emotional attachments are from our previous judgements. We cover them up with our body. We physically wear our convictions.

Listening to Roxy express her convictions affirmed Jai's feelings for her. He was becoming emotionally attached to this woman and he was enjoying it. She was letting him in more. She was letting down her barriers. They were laughing more and the encounters were uncovering a softer side to this very strong woman.

She then started in on his appearance. "Take you for example There's Island, Indian and I'd say British as well." He smiled and agreed. Not many picked up the British. "There is a possibility that as a British you were in their territory and as a brit would have patronised, intimidated abused and hated both Indian and Islanders. All the demeaning accusations others persecuted upon you as a child would have been the same expression you used to become the appearance of the person you are today." She thought that fascinating.

"Through your judgement or questioning in your previous life you are wearing the self-same hatred as your armour today, from your dark eyes to your hair to your physique. The same goes for obese people; they are hiding a cacophony of pain from previous lives. They are hiding their sexual pain and abuse; they are covering their hearts due to false belief systems that accused them of indecencies when they were innocent. Soldiers sexually abused women, children and babies, as they were accused by the church to be an abomination.

She gave him some names to look up as references for his book on how men had supposedly treated women. They identified them as vomit, excrement, bile's of humours; however what you have to also realise is both male and female have experienced both side of the fence and have participated in the abuse and the perpetration of the abuse, so although it is a male misogynistic dominant society both male and female have alternated to both sides so no one is entirely free.

Jai was pleased she cleared that up for she would have sounded like a man hater, but by donning that both genders have participated in the genocide of the sexes, she exonerated her view point and showed she understands the balance required.

Jai used this information and looked up the references and was appalled at the accusations to these genteel sexes. This material was giving him more than extra information, he checked his history and his philosophy and they all aligned with Roxy's references. She was filling him with a new enthusiasm to teach again. This book couldn't get finish soon enough.

He wanted to share her information with the world; she was inspirational to him.

Meanwhile Roxy was continuing her regression sessions with Jesse. Her latest one placed her as a male in vengeful warrior mode. She was filled with intense hatred and anger and she slayed Jai and his best friend twice in two different lifetimes. She showed no mercy and wanted to do it again.

Men needed to pay for their barbarism and she was doing it. She was a female in male form fighting for retribution. She wanted to go back further to find out why. When would this finish? Would she ever find the truth?

Jesse who had heard Jai's vision of him being with her had not arisen yet. He knew there was more so he was pushing her to find that one. It would tell an answer. At no time did he tell her of his experience, but she was losing interest so he was hanging on to this information as his last resort.

Jai did his seminar utilising the talents of her staff as the caterers and it proved to be very successful. Jason returned with the truck and unpacked the cold food then put the catering truck away and went inside with the day's takings; very successful day all round. He heard Jai's performance was exciting and the audience were all empowered.

Roxy, Jason and the seminar staff sat down to unwind and have a coffee when Jason saw Jai at the glass door. He invited him in and gave him a chai and they all sat down discussing the day's events. It must have been 4 in the morning when they all decided to leave. Staffs were rostered on to arrive at 5.30 and they didn't want to bump into the night staff.

Jai kissed Roxy on the cheek and thanked her for her assistance, then quietly left. He wanted more but felt it awkwardly inappropriate. He could sleep late in the morning but found himself too excited and too high to sleep.

Roxy worked from midday onward on the Sunday and was exhausted, but she had Monday off and this would be her last regression. She was getting too tired.

She informed Jesse of her decision so he decided to inform her of Jai's experience when they touched and he wanted to find that. She agreed that it may have the answers. As Jai wasn't a client this information wasn't confidential, it was gossip and that was fine by Jesse. He loved a little salacious gossip.

Roxy became comfortable and due to her tiredness went deep very quickly. She almost fell asleep; Jesse had to retrieve her. He asked her questions about her soul mate. She answered them and comfortably returned to a period where she was strong and Celtic. She told of a story of a betrothal that went wrong and she wound up marrying the groom who was her soul mate instead of her sister's.

On the wedding night he had to breathe her. They had to touch each other with their mouths but not kiss. They had to intertwine their hands and finger in the soul clutch. They would caress each other hands until they opened each other's soul by caressing the very centre of each other's hands. They then joined the souls together with the rings of gold for all eternity. Only then they were able to consummate the marriage body and soul. Roxy could feel her sexual stimulation exploding inside her as she spoke. She adored him completely.

They advanced forward, about 7 years, when civil war broke out. She lost her husband and her home. Her brother in law who was her husband's friend and her vengeful sister stole her home and left her desolate. She was pack raped by the paid usurpers and she died. With every painful violation, she swore vengeance. She swore by her soul she would take revenge to all filthy men as she died. She was filled with unforgiving hatred for all males and she would get retribution and her husband's friend would be at the top of the list.

Jesse woke her up. Her breathing seemed short. He told her to relax and breathe normally, which she did. He let her rest until she could rise completely. He explained that this was the one they needed. This one would explain all the pain that kept them apart. It could also explain why there was still an attraction between them.

She went home and fell asleep on her bed, extremely exhausted. It had been a full week. She decided to take the next couple of days off.

Over the next week it was business as usual and the only refreshing nuance in her life was Jai's visit to the café. They were regularly swapping ideas and philosophies. Jai was opening up to someone who understood and was able to elaborate and influence his opinions. He was able to exchange ideas, and expound more expressively on new ideas. She found herself experiencing sensual tension whenever he turned up and she was addressing it with a feminine expression in her attire.

CHAPTER 20

ROXY'S PRIVATE PAIN

Tension rose when Roxy didn't turn up for work; and she hadn't phoned. Jason was worried; he went round to her house there was no answer. He found the spare key under her flowerpot and entered calling Roxy's name. He ventured into her bedroom and saw she was having difficulty breathing. He called the ambulance and swiftly she was rushed to the hospital with minor heart palpitations.

Jason rang the studio looking Jai but the phone went to Jesse. Jesse went in to inform Jai Roxy was in hospital; Jai was confused. He didn't know Jesse knew Roxy. Jesse didn't want to get involved. Jai wanted answers, but now wasn't the time. He arrived at hospital information centre and they informed him she was in ICU and he, not being family, was not allowed to enter.

He waited outside her room extremely anxious. No one would tell him anything about her. Jesse arrived with Roxy's file. Jai wanted answers. Jesse explained the situation and told him Roxy said if the need arises, he could read her file now that she knew all the answers. He didn't realise it would be so soon.

Jesse left him alone but before he left, he told him how Roxy felt about him and went back to the studio. The words "she loves you" echoed through Jai's head. He had to know more. Jesse asked Gary to assist at the big studio if he had the time. Jai didn't want to read her chart he wanted to see her, but that wasn't going to happen so he started reading out of frustration. It took him about two and half hours. The patterns melded together like a continuum should.

As he read, he saw a menagerie of entangled unwarrantable injustices. Now we are here and he was going to lose her again. A nurse who was a friend came over and sat beside him to console him. She said she couldn't discuss the case but she could tell him that her daughter would be arriving the next day. Maybe he could talk to her. She took his number and said she would call him if there was any change. She then urged him to go home and get some rest.

He went home, but rest was out of the question. When morning came, he realises they wouldn't let him in until she could have visitors, so he went to work and tried to maintain focus. Gary assisted him and Jesse with appointments, and they both let Jai do the simple ones. Late in the afternoon he wanted to phone to see if there was any change, but Jesse convinced him to let it go; stressing out was not going to help. The hospital would call if there was any change, so at Jesse's recommendation Jai went and did a deep meditation.

It was another restless night; he was starting to realise how much she meant to him, and now to find out they were soul mates opened a floodgate of emotions he never knew he had. He wanted to hold her and never let her go. Would she let him? Would she feel the same? This was torment. When the hospital finally rang, they informed him he could see her at visiting hours. He saw the daughter with her mother and she beckoned him to come in.

A nurse had explained that Jai was a friend and he would like to talk to her. Val, the daughter was excited to meet Jai as she was an avid fan. However, Jai was more interested in Roxy.

Apparently, her mother's heart condition was an affliction from birth. She explained how it was time for her mother to move close to her so she could be taken care of. Val personally didn't have time but she would make arrangements to have her placed in a home close by where they could take care of her in her fragile condition.

When her mother recovered a bit more, she would return to her home town and make arrangements to have her bought back home three hours away.

Jai listened as he saw his life and Roxy's life fall apart, word by word. He may not have known her as long as her daughter, but he was sure she would want to stay there. This was her home now; but Roxy's daughter was adamant that Roxy would have to leave.

When Jai visited the hospital the next day Roxy was placed in her own ward. He was able to see her by himself. She was still very tired. He sat with her and took her hand and kissed the back of it tenderly and held it against his face. Roxy whispered; "Did you know Louis the 14th was known as the king who touch the hearts of thousands of women in France."

Jai looked up and "shh, you shouldn't be talking." But Roxy kept on whispering. "He would sensually kiss the back of their hands then if he wanted them to come to him that night; he would kiss the inside of their wrist and tongue kiss their palm." She paused and caught her breath. King Henry the eighth left all the women of England he touched, with syphilis."

Jai laughed and kissed her hand again; she dosed off again. He sat and watched her for hours. He wasn't going to lose her again. She was funny, smart and brilliant. He would take her home with him. He had a spare room. If she wanted it and he would love to take care of her until other arrangements were made, her arrangements. This idea was perfect for him. He only hoped she would want to. It was impromptu but he was sure he could help her.

As she recovered, she told him this was something that happens when she gets too tired. Her daughter was as always over reacting. She had always looked at her mother as dead man walking and Roxy hated it. He informed her of his solution and told her to think about it; it was there if she wanted it.

Her daughter arrived back and was anxious to return to work, but she had made arrangements to have her mother moved the next day. She would have to stay with her daughter until a room became available. Roxy informed the nurse to ring Jai about the arrangements. She wanted to stay.

The next morning both Roxy and Val were checking out. Jai entered the front doors and walked straight up to Roxy. He took her out of the wheel chair to stand in front of him. He held her for the first time and gazed deeply into her eyes. He smiled for now he knew she wanted this too. It was easy. He held her with his right arm and ran his hand down her left arm as if grasping her hand for a dance. He held it palm to palm in the soul hold.

"Do you want to go home with Val or come home with me?" he asked. Val started to object. Roxy held her breath as she smiled at him. "I'll take care of you," then he kissed her gently on the lips, she raised her arms up around his neck and kissed him back, she said nothing. He wrapped his arm around her and took her to his waiting car outside the front door. Val stood in shock as she and the nurse watched them both depart without a word. The nurse lowered her head as she smiled in agreement of what she saw.

Not a word was spoken as he drove her to his house and placed her luggage into the spare room. He opened a shade to let in some light. She slowly straddled in behind him. He returned to her and then he stood in front of her and kissed her. He spoke to her and she answered, but once he kissed her, he couldn't stop. He guided her to his bed then he lay beside her and constantly kissing her and she counteracted so easily. "You need to take it easy." She grinned. "Uh huh" she responded as she came back for more. They embraced, kissed and loved in length, and then her mobile rang. Jai left the room to get it for her. He exited the room so she could talk. He went into her room and opened it up and let in some more light and air then returned to his room when there was silence. He asked if she had a robe, and then went to get it for her.

He lay beside her again, caressing her, then he questioned, "You sure you want this?"

She queried, "You?"

He felt himself bringing her closer to him as he could feel her breath enticing his lips "More than anything else" She found herself embracing him from top to bottom, body and soul totally engulfing his being.

"No more mystery, it is finally clear to me; it is you I have loved all along" she whispered.

There were things that had to be done but for now they were exactly where they wanted to be and nothing else mattered. Nights turned into days and days turned into weeks. Roxy regained her strength and Jai had a lot of new ideas he wanted to try out.

He decided to become a fulltime author, with seminars. He wanted to write about their love and life; he wanted to give his share of the studio to Gary his son. This was when Roxy encountered Alex for the first time and realised, he was the one who betrayed Jai and took everything from her. They passed each other at the door of the studio so their meeting was short, but she felt an enormous darkness around him and they never saw each other again.

Jai wanted to spend all the time with his loving Roxy, and being an author would allow him to stay at home with her. Roxy wanted to go back to work so they agreed she could oversee all the elements of the restaurant and do whatever she was capable of doing. However, there would be limitations. No more really late nights, and when she felt tired, she was to rest.

After Jai gave his studio to his son, Roxy asked if she should leave her café to Jason. Jai said it was hers to do with as she liked. Roxy pointed out that if she was to stay with Jai, he would automatically receive the café. Jai didn't want the cafe; but he liked the idea of it staying in the bay. That gave Jai the courage to do what he really wanted to do.

He had a friend who designed jewellery. He knew Roxy loved onyx, and he knew she wanted to reconnect with Jai as her soul mate so he asked his friend to create two wedding rings one male one female of the yin yang sign in black and white onyx. When they were finished, he had a plan. He prepared a special dinner and Jai asked her to marry him; He wanted her body and soul again now and into the next life, not in the next life only. Roxy now knew she wanted the same. If they could have the ultimate relationship now, their future lives would be secure.

21
CHAPTER

HERE COMES THE BRIDE

Next up was the how, when and where. Neither wanted a wedding, so the pier sounded perfect and the café for the breakfast. They had to go the registry office first then they asked family and all her friends mostly staff and customers to celebrate with them on the pier. Jai had Jesse, Gary, Jason and Jonah. It was small but those who shared their life were invited to the ceremony. It was a double ring ceremony and Jason excelled with the reception. Their loving relationship was quickly becoming the talk of the town in respect to their happiness. Jai always had his arms around her and she with him.

Jai was having difficulty writing his book. He had so much to say and it wouldn't unravel in his head. Roxy's teachings played an important part in his book.

Roxy informed him that she had to be in the place of unbelievable love in her mind, body and soul long before she came to the bay. Roxy had already created the path long before she could walk it. She compared it to the ring of her dreams.

Roxy would say Jai's eyes were like pure onyx; deep pools of nothingness with endless possibilities, simply looking into them and her entire inner soul would sensually awaken her entire body. They held the keys to the universe.

The Onyx stone was a symbol of the love between them. To acquire the ring, she had to realise she has already received it. Rumi states that "*what you are looking for is looking for you.*" By doing this you are opening the pathway to what is rightfully yours.

Along the path you will see several onyx rings and this is informing you that you are on the right path. Finally, before your eyes will be the ring of your dreams. You'll ask and question. You'll go home and think about it and you won't be able to get it out of your mind. You'll have to return to see it again. You have to have it. You have to buy it. This is how it occurs with all things including love.

Roxy explained to Jai "long before I came here, I wanted to find the love that I deserved to have. The one I wanted more than life itself. I saw the café and I fell in love with it and then I met Jason and Jonah. Their love was the one I wanted. I knew I was on the right path because they were displaying the ultimate love I wanted to experience before me. Every time they shared their love with me, I became so happy knowing I was on the right path.

You came in and I had to test the waters with Jesse and find out more and I did. It unfolded the most amazing love story to be shared by two people. We nearly destroyed each other, but when we were together, nothing compared. This is what I wanted years ago. But here is the amazing part.

We started this journey over 1900 years ago, but when we focus and don't lose balance; all doors open in the most amazing love ever experienced. I didn't want anything less. When you came for me at the hospital there was no turning back; you were my black onyx, my forever loving pool of endless probabilities. They are like the deepest depth of the ocean. We cannot see in but you can see everything."

I always wanted this for my next life. I never really expected it to occur in this one. That's why you don't ask. When we ask, we put timelines and restriction on it, but by not asking it's open and I got it much earlier than I expected.

Roxy explained further so he could write it in his book. That's what every woman wants. Men want football; we need to teach the women to alter their attitudes so they can have much more than football, pies and racing cars. Once women start creating from the very love that emanates from them and if they don't become caught up in the nesting impulses, they can have amazing experiences; they don't deserve less, they deserve it all. We all deserve it all."

Roxy's passion to be loved extended from all her past lives; however, what exacerbated her pain here was her own life experience. It was informing her of all her past life pains that had to be rectified before she could move on. Every lifetime was telling her of the immense pain caused when her soul is divided and is torn apart.

Roxy was born imperfect to a mother who could not abide imperfection. She would beat Roxy to make her stronger, least that is what she told her. Roxy was born Rosa, and her mother altered to name to rocks, meaning hard as stone. The name Roxy stuck. She married an abusive husband and her daughter is also hard as stone. All the love and joy in Roxy's life was beaten out of her.

Then she recognised that she had done this to herself in her past lives so she had to alter her opinion of herself; love those who were informing her of her disposition and create a new Roxy; create a new path for Roxy. As she did things around her began to alter. She felt braver to try new ideas. She stepped out of the usual and ventured against everyone else's wishes.

She knew that if she stayed nothing would change, so she changed it. Look at what she achieved by knowing she truly loved herself. She could attract the same love to her. She had to love her as much as she would love him and that love had to be inside of her before she could find him, and it worked. She was now the happiest she has ever been in centuries and it was just beginning.

Jai had to write all this down; she was his story, she lived how we should walk toward our true destiny. We were never meant to be alone. This oneness is about being one with the love of all our lives; once we find them the rest of life echoes back to us through it. It's not the people, it's the love, the emotion.

You can't walk alone, it's empty. You will only receive half of your true destiny in material form. Knowing that you can share this love with the other side of your soul completes you and from there you are limitless and ageless.

She still held that magic in her hands and her voice. Her passion for their love showed no bounds and when she spoke Jai fell in love with her over and over again. She was like a music box with millions of melodies all rendering beauty through her soul.

He found enormous pleasure in simply holding her, embracing her, and being with her sharing her exuberance for even existing with him. He could feel her love for him was unlocking more and more of his love for her. She was a mesmerising mystique.

He wanted to write about all of his feelings but he had always been a very stoic logical person. These emotions need adjectives and emotional words to express how she was making him feel and they didn't come easily. How do you write a book with words that don't exist? This was his conundrum.

They went everywhere together and he became one of those people who could not let her hand or body go. He had to have his arm around her. He felt incomplete without her. He became one of those people he used to envy, the people who knew the truth. The ones who didn't have to struggle to acquire anything because they knew they already had it.

Every moment for the next twelve years was this immense feeling of bliss. He would ask why she had to leave him behind, and she would say he has work to finish; but she will never leave him she will always be with him. He wasn't allowed to give up this time. He had to look for her. She would always be there. He simply had to find her.

He started doing seminars with her. She would do platform; that meant she would express herself in the middle of the seminar and he would start and complete it. They became very popular with their sexual innuendo's and double meanings. They always spoke from experience and many times Jai would use purposeful anecdote of their life together to help audiences comprehend that this life was real and within their grasp.

They averaged two seminars per year and several guest appearances and this is how they made their money together.

This is how the universe rewarded them and supplied them with everything they needed while they were together.

CHAPTER 22

WRETCHED HEARTACHE

One Sunday morning as Jai woke and went to make breakfast, Roxy lay quietly in bed and then screamed. Jai dropped everything and ran to her. He called the ambulance. He held her, but she didn't re awaken. NO! NO! NO! The moment he dreaded was here. He wasn't ready, not now. He felt a huge tear in his entire body. He held her as he rocked back and forth. He felt she had been torn from him like his skin had been torn from his body.

The next few weeks were a blur of unimaginable pain. He couldn't stay in their bed. He preferred to be away from the house, the café anywhere that reminded him of her He knew what she had said but this pain was unbearable. The pain is supposed to ease with time but it wasn't doing that, it was getting worse. He'd lost his heart beat; he'd lost her heart beat. The beat he had was only belting out pain.

He had her urn of her ashes and he was to scatter them across the bay. He lit a small bonfire and he stood at the edge of the water for hours before he had the courage to scatter them. His world was shattered. In the background the café played her favourite songs. He heard the songs and fell into the sand in a crumbled heap and bawled in anguish. It was as if the song was the message tearing him apart. He stayed there in the cold for what seemed hours until Jesse came looking for him. He picked him up and took him back to his place. He reeked with pain and curled up into a ball and fell asleep.

Days turned into weeks and he felt he needed to get out. He couldn't write here, he couldn't think. He needed to get some air. He would go to the bay to see if she was there but there was nothing.

He packed his things ready to leave. Finally, he decided to go to the bay to say goodbye one last time. As usual the café was playing some of Roxy's favourite songs. He listened and started crying like a child.

It was late and he was talking quietly. Then the talking mirrored his horrific pain anguish and distress. Out of complete frustration he screamed to the sky with his arms outstretched "you said you'd never leave me. What do you want from me?" he paused for some breath. "Geez Roxy I love you; I love you so much I can't do this" then as he tried to stand to go home. "Flamin' hell woman, I do still love you I do but this wretched pain it won't stop."

Roxy heard his voice yelling from the other side. She came running across the bay of water to him as fast as she could. She ran straight into him and knocked him over. She started kissing him but he couldn't feel it. He sat up unimpressed at the huge gust of wind that came from out of nowhere and threw him into the air.

She sat in front of him "I love you too" she said as he said "thanks I love you too" in sarcastic condescension. Roxy sat there in front of him staring into his ebony eyes, twisting her fingers, hoping he heard her. His head stopped for a second, "you heard me. Tell me you heard me" Roxy started anxiously saying. The penny dropped. He repeated the words, "I love you too" and Roxy jumped on top of him and started kissing him all over. He lay back on the sand, he thought, "my god you're here. You're in everything. You're all around me." he blasted with enlightened happiness.

"Figure it out. Yes, you've got it" she exclaimed as she started kissing him again on the sand. "I'm here. I will never leave you my love, ever" she whispered in his ear. "But you did this, not me please figure it out" she waited. "Please figure it out or I'll have to go."

He felt love within him again. The pain was dissolving. He was able to look at everything that reminded him of her and realise she left them here for him to remain close to her, not the other way around. If he clung to the love he created, they created, they would never be separated, it was his choice because the love made them one.

He lay there for a long while absorbing all this new information. If he remained in love with her, he would never lose her. He could create that love; it was his choice. He didn't want to lose her again. He didn't talk, he lay quiet. He simply let all this tsunami of information come to him. It was their love all around him, she was talking and kissing him and running her finger through his hair. He could feel her touching him. He felt this love within him growing, so he doubled it, "now my darling, you are with me forever and ever and ever" He smile at his creative ingeniousness.

He went home and started writing about this love and as he wrote he imagined, she stood behind him with her arms around his neck, touching his hair, kissing his neck, loving him. He would walk down to the bay and he'd feel her presence in everything there. Her hands combing through his hair as the wind blew, her hand in his, he felt it all. But more than anything else he was intensely happy. He had just lost his wife and he was intensely happy remembering everything about her. It was like when you first start creating the love of your life and you don't know who she or he is, only he knows who she is, and she is waiting for him to come home.

Val was starting trouble about the restaurant for she believed Jai only married her mother to get her property. So, Jai gave her the money then sold Roxy's rental house for reimbursement.

Then the café was reverted to Jason, as Roxy wanted, without any hang ups. He was ecstatic. With all the challenging going on Jason imagined he'd be out of work. He was too old to start again. He loved it there in the restaurant, on the bay. When he received the news from the lawyer that it was all his no questions asked, he and Jonah were over joyed.

After thirteen years Alex his promoter, had met with some maleficence which took everyone by surprise especially Jai. Frank the detective abused Jai for his seminars accusing him of disrupting relationships only to become one of Jai's love victims with his wife. Jai could see their loving touch was working everywhere.

However, Jai was now short a promotions manager.

At the café, Jason asked; "do you think she's still here, because I'm getting these incredibly inspirational ideas of new savoury cakes." Jai laughed, "oh yeah; and I'd do those cakes too or else' he laughed with a friendly warning.

"Oh, incidentally this guy left his card for you. He does media promotions." Her little café still had her amazing touch and their love was working on everyone in the valley with it including Jai. "Thank you beautiful," he whispered he sat in his usual seat. He imagined her saying "You're welcome lovely" as she kissed his head.

His book and the new promotional team stretched Jai and Roxy's message further than he could have ever imagined. He loved his story of his love for his angel, who stayed with him till the end. She would be on the stage with him laughing as usual. She never left him and when he visited her at the bay Roxy was there with him, beside him holding on to him with her head on his shoulder

On the day he passed away Roxy was at the top of the stairs waiting for him to return. When he returned, he took her in his arms and the universe exploded like the skies at New Year's Eve as he finally received his heart's desire for all the loving knowledge, he shared to the world of his unconditional love for his soul mate.

It is in the giving that you will receive. Giving to others unconditionally and you will receive your heart's desire.

CHAPTER 23

WELCOME HOME JAI

Jai and his friends now started to utilise the chess gazebo and this enticed others to join them again. The council created more tables for them to play and maintained the gardens and shade. This was progress in the bay at a pace Jai and his friends enjoyed. Jason became one of the regulars and he still supplied the coffee for all his friends.

They all laughed, played, watched the young swim and try to surf in the water and this was how they shared their retirement. In the colder months many of the older ones were kept inside out of the cold but not Jai. The nurses had wrap him up to bring him down if only for a few minutes to say hello to his loving Roxy.

"Mr Tagore we'll have to go in soon it's getting colder" said one of his nurses, as she pulled up his warm blanket.

"Not yet please" was his response.

"Five more minutes then," she quietly whispered.

"Not long now love; five more minutes." With that he quietly breathed his last. His hand slipped down the side of his wheelchair and his head slumped forward. Jesse saw and came running and shouting his name as fast as he could and the nurse called the ambulance.

Jai stepped out of his body; still an old man and he looked back on the scene that beheld him. An old man slumped in a chair with panic and bedlam all around him. He started floating toward the bay.

Jesse was standing up behind his chair and looking in his direction with tears in his eyes.

He raised his hand slightly up to wave good bye to his best friend as if he could see him, "give her our love and say hello to her for me. Good bye old friend, I'll see you soon." Then he turned back to his friend's body.

Jai turned away from the scene and looked forward into the bay. A stair case appeared in front of him.

He laughed and gave a heavy sigh, "great" he reacted in humorous disgust. "Everybody else gets a high-speed vortex, an elevator, a chasm; trust me to get the staircase."

Feeling his age at the bottom of the stairs he started to struggled up the steps and as he rose, his age disappeared and by the time he reached the top, he was his prime beautiful self again; strong, healthy and fit.

In front of him was an endless cloud; this was not the scene he expected. He asked "where am I?"

Her beautiful melodic voice resounded through the emptiness, "This is your creation."

Recognising her tuneful voice "Where are you?" he searchingly questioned looking through the air trying to find her in anticipation.

"In front of you," she answered as her hologram revealed his magnificent love in human form before him. He took her in his arms, caressed her face looked deeply into her eyes and smiled and felt the warmth of her love flowing through him. His entire body smiled.

"Welcome home" she whispered as she blissfully kisses him while enjoying the wondrous embrace of his scanning hands all over her body.

He kisses her face, her lips and progresses to her neck as she curls and sighs in his embrace. He then looks into her eyes and grins and laughs under his breath.

"What are you laughing at?" Roxy queries

"There's nobody here. I have no more past life victimising memories in front of me. My cluster, all the people who were my feedback of all my past pain, none of them are here. He gazes lustfully in her eyes and slowly whispers, "except you."

She smiles back at him. "yes, I know, you released them all. You are genuinely free, and you didn't die with any allegiances or past regrets. You allowed them all to exist without you."

He holds her for a while, then he starts laughing. So, it is true.

"What's true?" she asks

"Nirvana to nirvana?"

"She smiles; "it is simply what you perceive it to be."

He laughs, "this is my perception? This is my perception, my imagination my creation?" He laughs even louder.

"You know what I love about this place?"

Roxy curiously grins back and shakes her head.

He slowly combs his hand through her hair to draw her lips nearer to his, as he sensually whispers.

THIS IS WHAT IT IS ALL ABOUT;
THIS IS WHAT WE STRIVE FOR;
NEUTRAL; EQUAL
YOU; ME; AS ONE

With that he rolls her down into the clouds.

"I have missed loving you so much."

After a long period of magical love making Roxy sighs,

"Wow, what do you want to do now?" She laughs.

Jai glides over on top of her and in his very low sensual voice whispers as he starts kissing her body, "THIS"

NOW THAT'S NIRVANA!

WHAT'S NIRVANA?

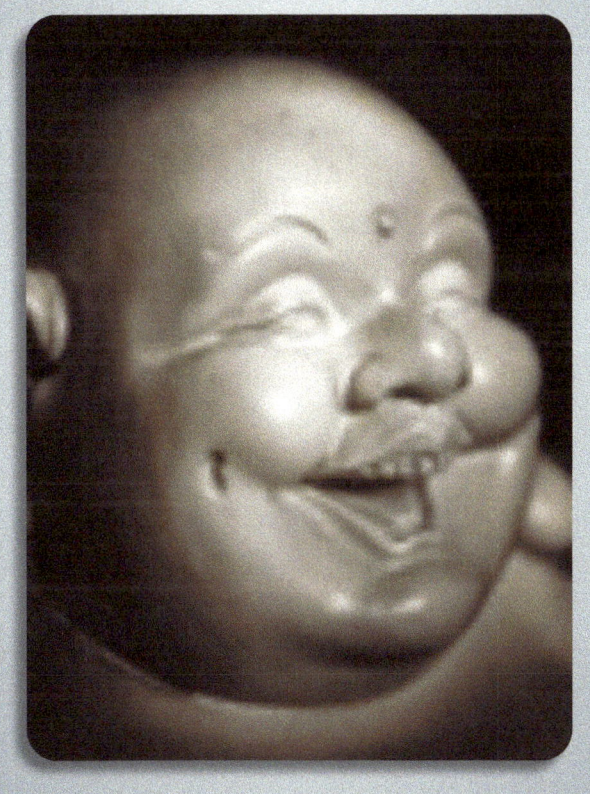

DON'T ASK!

INDEX OF IMAGES
PIXABAY

integration-3527268___340 face binary network pixabay page 17

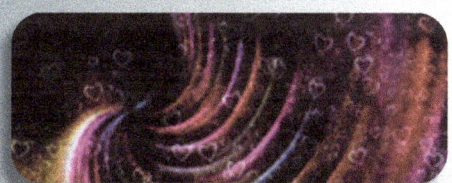

bokeh-4241714___340 magical pixabay page 1

green-692079___340 grass tree pixabay page 4.

galaxy-382204__340pixabay universe woman.jpg

Jesus-3507364__340 Jesus Christ pixabay

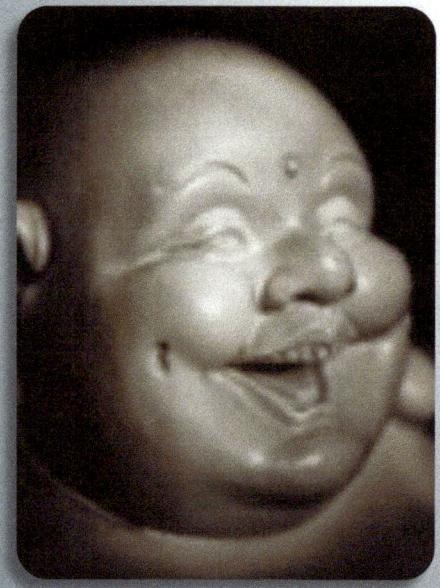
buddha-750132__340 laughing 17 spirituality pixabay.jpg

Thankyou
And
Good night.

www.ingramcontent.com/pod-product-compliance
Lightning Source LLC
Chambersburg PA
CBHW041126110526
44592CB00020B/2705